THE
INFORTUNATE

Also by Susan E. Klepp:

The "Swift Progress of Population": A Documentary and Bibliographic Study of Philadelphia's Growth, 1642–1859

Philadelphia in Transition: A Demographic History of the City and Its Occupational Groups, 1720–1830

Also edited by Susan E. Klepp:

Souls for Sale: The Autobiographies of Two German Redemptioners, with Farley Grubb and Anne Pfaelzer de Ortiz

Demographic History of the Philadelphia Region, 1600–1860

Also by Billy G. Smith:

Encyclopedia of American History: Colonization and Settlement, 1685–1763

The "Lower Sort": Philadelphia's Laboring People, 1750–1800

Also edited by Billy G. Smith:

Down and Out in Early America

"A Melancholy Scene of Devastation": The Public Response to the 1793 Philadelphia Yellow Fever Epidemic, with J. Worth Estes

Life in Early Philadelphia: Documents from the Revolutionary and Early National Periods

Blacks Who Stole Themselves: Advertisements for Runaways in the Pennsylvania Gazette, 1728–1790, with Richard Wojtowicz

The

INFORTUNATE

The Voyage and Adventures of

WILLIAM MORALEY,

an Indentured Servant

SECOND EDITION

Edited with an Introduction and Notes by

SUSAN E. KLEPP

&

BILLY G. SMITH

The Pennsylvania State University Press
University Park, Pennsylvania

Library of Congress Cataloging-in-Publication Data

Moraley, William, 18th cent.
    The infortunate : the voyage and adventures of William Moraley, an
indentured servant / edited with an introduction and notes by
Susan E. Klepp & Billy G. Smith.– 2nd ed.
        p.   cm.
    Originally published: Newcastle, 1743. With new introd.
    Includes bibliographical references and index.
    ISBN 0-271-02676-6 (alk. paper)
    1. Pennsylvania—Social life and customs—To 1775.   2. Moraley, William, 18th
cent.   3. Indentured servants—Pennsylvania—Biography.   I. Klepp, Susan E.
II. Smith, Billy Gordon.   III. Title.

F152.M78   2005
917.4804′2—dc22   2005048852

Published by The Pennsylvania State University Press,
University Park, PA 16802-1003
Printed in the United States of America

First edition published in 1992
Reprinted six times

The Pennsylvania State University Press is a member of the
Association of American University Presses.

It is the policy of The Pennsylvania State University Press to use acid-free paper. Publications
on uncoated stock satisfy the minimum requirements of American National Standard for Information Sciences—Permanence of Paper for Printed Library Materials, ANSI Z39.48-1992.

*For Jack Leon Smith, Sage Adrienne Smith, Edith Klepp Mueser,
L. S. Klepp, and Maggie Klepp*

CONTENTS

LIST OF ILLUSTRATIONS

Maps

Figures

EDITORS' PREFACE TO THE SECOND EDITION

We are very pleased to issue a second edition of William Moraley's *The Infortunate*, with a substantially rewritten introduction and a new Afterword. This edition is designed primarily to help students and teachers in university, college, and high-school courses to read and interpret this rare memoir of an eighteenth-century indentured servant. The first edition of the autobiography has been widely assigned in classes and also used extensively by scholars to address a host of issues about colonial America. We have drawn on our own pedagogical experience and on valuable suggestions from other educators to devise a more "teachable" edition of the volume. We rewrote the introduction to contain less interpretative material and more of the basic information necessary to help readers understand the memoir on their own. We also added a number of questions intended to direct attention to vital issues, including new ones about globalization and the Atlantic World that have assumed greater importance since the first edition appeared a dozen years ago.

An Afterword suggests analytical approaches to the memoir and new information about Moraley based on recently discovered evidence. Working in British archives and libraries and with newly available Internet sources, we learned new details about Moraley's circumstances in both Newcastle and London that have a bearing on his decision to sell himself into servitude in North America. In addition, we uncovered a good deal more about Moraley's life after he returned to Newcastle, much of which sheds light on why he wrote the memoir. We also found that Moraley published several more short works, one of which is still extant and provides insights into his political views. This new material should provide readers new tools with which to decipher Moraley and his times.

We continue to believe this memoir provides a remarkable view of the life and times of one "ordinary" person. It is the kind of account required to help us comprehend the past and the present not only from the perspective of the rich and famous but also from the standpoint of those in the middling and lower ranks of society who made significant, lasting contributions to constructing our own world.

Our thanks to Montana State University, Temple University, the late John Philipson of the Newcastle Society of Antiquaries, David E. Schoonover, Curator of Rare Books, University of Iowa Special Collections, and the many readers and commentators on the first edition.

EDITORS' PREFACE TO THE FIRST EDITION

Eighteenth-century America has been called the Age of Benjamin Franklin, an era best characterized by the values expressed in his autobiography and by his incredibly successful career. Yet Franklin was only one of several million inhabitants of the North American colonies, and by his own account he was both exceptionally hardworking and unusually fortunate.

But what if his luck had been different? What if Franklin's father had not acceded to his son's occupational choice, if the young runaway apprentice had been apprehended by authorities, if several well-established printers had dominated the trade in Philadelphia when Franklin arrived, if his creditors had sued to collect his debts, if his wife's first husband had returned and charged him with bigamy, if fornication charges had been brought at the birth of his illegitimate son, if illness or a large family had drained his resources, or if the local economy had stagnated at critical junctures in his career? Had any of these things happened, Franklin might well have been just another obscure artisan, invisible to all but the most persistent scholars.

"smart, sassy, and articulate"

During the last two decades, historians have expanded the scope of history by attempting to recover the experiences and contributions of the forgotten and less fortunate inhabitants of Britain and its American colonies. It is a difficult task, because so few artisans, laborers, sailors, slaves, and women left firsthand accounts of their lives. The editors of this volume have spent most of their academic careers analyzing tax lists, church registers, newspaper reports, probate records, and census schedules in an effort to recreate some of the daily physical experiences—including family, health, diet, income, housing, and work—of the middling and laboring residents of the eighteenth-century Mid-Atlantic region. But the thoughts, beliefs, hopes, and opinions of the majority remain elusive, even as our knowledge of their objective conditions has increased.

After toiling in the archives for years only to find scattered scraps of evidence, what a pleasure it was to discover the autobiography of William Moraley. Smart, sassy, and articulate, Moraley provides a considerably richer view of common experience in the eighteenth-century Anglo-American world than do most other sources. His memoirs depict the life of a down-and-out artisan whose fortune, like that of so many other immigrant bound workers, did not substantially improve. The autobiography also offers a complex perspective that can be read on numerous levels. In particular, it reflects the enigmas of the eighteenth-century Atlantic world in a series of unsettling juxtapositions: science and superstition, religion and roguery, industry and indulgence, fact and fiction, heroic ambition and humble subservience.

In many ways William Moraley lived out the worst-case scenario for eighteenth-century artisans. What succeeded for Franklin failed for Moraley. While Franklin marched from triumph to triumph, Moraley reeled from one misfortune to another. Was Moraley truly unfortunate or merely feckless? The reasons for the different career paths of men in the lower classes have been the subject of much scholarly debate. Moraley's memoirs can more firmly ground that controversy in actual human experience and contribute to our understanding of the eighteenth-century Atlantic world.

Just as history has often failed to credit those not in the limelight for their vital contributions to shaping the past and the present, so too do the conventions of authorship frequently obscure the cooperative and communal nature of historical research and writing. This preface allows a conventional, if less than fully adequate, opportunity to express our gratitude for the generosity, insight, and expertise of others.

Unlike Moraley, we have been very fortunate in pursuing this enterprise, and we wish to thank Farley Grubb, P. M. G. Harris, Bernard Herman, Craig Horle, Judy McGaw, Tom Slaughter, Marianne Wokeck, Michael Zuckerman, and members of the seminar of the Philadelphia [now McNeil] Center for Early American Studies for their comments on the Introduction. The following people and institutions also kindly provided us with invaluable assistance: the Burlington County Historical Society and Rhett Pernot, Dorothy Eckert, and Kathy Heuer; Bert Denker and the staff at the Winterthur Museum and Library; Roy Goodman at the American Philosophical Society; Philip Lapsansky at the Library Company of Philadelphia; Dr. J. M. Fewster and Mrs. J. L. Drury of the Division of Archives and Special Collections of the University of Durham Library; Patricia Sheldon of the Newcastle Central Library and Constance M. Fraser of the Society of Antiquaries of Newcastle upon Tyne; and the staffs at the Genealogical Society of Pennsylvania, the Historical Society of Pennsylvania, Van Pelt Library at the University of Pennsylvania, Moore Library at Rider College, and the Family History Library of the Church of Jesus Christ of Latter-Day Saints in Broomall, Pennsylvania. The William Clements Library at the University of Michigan granted permission to print the complete edition of Moraley's autobiography which is part of their holdings. A Mellon Fellowship at the American Philosophical Society and research support from Montana State University helped the editors complete this book. Betty Smith and Richard Wojtowicz assisted in preparing the manuscript. And Peter Potter, the editor at Penn State Press, provided much needed encouragement and very helpful suggestions. We also gratefully acknowledge the support of our families throughout this project.

ABBREVIATIONS

AIS   Roland Vern Jackson, comp., *Early New Jersey, 1600–1819* (Bountiful, Utah: Accelerated Indexing Systems, 1981). Photo offset of computer-generated genealogical abstracts from the Family History Library of the Church of Jesus Christ of Latter-Day Saints.

GSP   Genealogical Society of Pennsylvania, housed at the Historical Society of Pennsylvania, Philadelphia.

IGI   International Genealogical Index, Church of Jesus Christ of Latter-Day Saints. Microfiche of computer-generated genealogical abstracts. Copies at the Family History Center, Pennsylvania Stake, Broomall, Pennsylvania. The origins and a description of this collection are available in Alex Shoumatoff, *A Mountain of Names* (New York: Simon & Schuster, 1985), esp. 227–93. Some of this material is now online; see http://www.family search.org/.

PMHB   *Pennsylvania Magazine of History and Biography.*

Wills   *New Jersey Archives,* First Series: *Documents Relating to the Colonial History of the State of New Jersey,* vols. 1–13, *Abstracts of Wills,* ed. A. Van Doren Honeyman (Somerville, N.J.: Unionist-Gazette, 1918).

EDITORS' INTRODUCTION

The comments and observations of European visitors have served as invaluable sources for our knowledge about early America.[1] However, wealthy travelers left most accounts, and they frequently saw the New World through the windows of fancy carriages and formed their opinions in conversations with the colonial elite. William Moraley's memoir, first published in 1743, offers a decidedly different perspective.

William Moraley (1699–1762) was born in London in 1699 (listed as 1698 in the "old style" calendar). He was trained in the law, but saw his legal education interrupted by a financial crisis. His family moved to Newcastle upon Tyne in the 1720s, where he was apprenticed to his father, a watchmaker. It was not a happy relationship. Moraley was disowned, moved back to London, and was soon impoverished. He then ventured to

---

1. Among the journals left by travelers in the Mid-Atlantic region are *The America of 1750: Peter Kalm's Travels in North America*, ed. Adolph B. Benson, 2 vols. (New York: Dover Publications, 1964); J. P. Brissot de Warville, *New Travels in the United States of America, 1788*, ed. and trans. Durand Escheverria and Mara Soceanu (Cambridge, Mass.: Harvard University Press, 1964); and Kenneth Roberts and Anna M. Roberts, eds., *Moreau de St. Mery's American Journey* [1793–1798] (Garden City, N.Y.: Doubleday, 1947).

the British American colonies in 1729 as an indentured servant, where he worked in various capacities, rambled about the countryside on foot, and mingled with white and black bondpeople, laborers, artisans, and other common folk, as well as prominent Indian and colonial figures.[2] He returned to Newcastle and eventually wrote an account of his life and travels. While the very act of writing makes Moraley unusual, his experiences resembled those of many eighteenth-century European migrants, the majority of whom sold themselves into bondage to secure transport to North America.[3]

Many journals, diaries, and letters by affluent early Americans survive, but autobiographies, wherein individuals reflect on the course and meaning of their lives, are rare. Benjamin Franklin's autobiography, written near the end of his exceptionally successful career, stands out as one of the few eighteenth-century American accounts.[4] More extraordinary still are memoirs of people like Moraley who stood on the bottom rungs of American society and who, unlike Franklin, were unable to ascend the social and economic ladder.[5]

2. The son of William Moraley and Martha Mason Moraley, William Moraley was born on February 25, 1699, and baptized four days later. (Throughout we have converted all years from the "old style" calendar, which began the year on March 1, to the "new style," where the year began in January.) Moraley's father initially had been apprenticed on September 7, 1691, to John Willoughby. He achieved his freedom in 1703 after having served for a dozen years learning the art and mystery of clockmaking. The office of the Archbishop of Canterbury in Knightrider Street, London, issued the marriage license for Moraley's parents on November 24, 1697. Moraley's birth and baptism are recorded in Willoughby A. Littledale, ed., *The Registers of Christ Church, Newgate, 1538 to 1754*, vol. 21 of *Publications of the Harleian Society—Registers*, 105 vols. (London: Harleian Society, 1895), 91. The apprenticeship of Moraley's father is recorded in Charles Edward Atkins, *Register of Apprentices of the Worshipful Company of Clockmakers of the City of London from Its Incorporation in 1631 to Its Tercentenary in 1931* (privately printed, 1931), 204. The date of the marriage license of Moraley's parents is in George E. Cokayne and Edward Alexander Fry, eds., *The Index Library: Calendar of Marriage Licenses Issued by the Faculty Office, 1632–1714* (London: By subscription, 1905), 153. William Moraley (the author of this memoir) was apprenticed to his father on May 5, 1718, as recorded in the Clockmakers Company, Court Minutes, Volume 3, Ms 2710/3, Guildhall Library and Manuscripts, London. He died and was buried in Newcastle's St. Nicholas churchyard on January 19, 1762, as recorded in M. A. Richardson, *The Local Historian's Table Book, of Remarkable Occurrences, Historical Facts, Traditions, Legendary and Descriptive Ballads, etc., etc., Connected with the Counties of Newcastle-upon-Tyne, Northumberland and Durham*, 8 vols. (Newcastle upon Tyne: Richardson, 1841), 2:104, and in the church records of St. Nicholas Church, Newcastle.

3. On eighteenth-century indentured servants, see David W. Galenson, *White Servitude in Colonial America: An Economic Analysis* (Cambridge: Cambridge University Press, 1981); Abbot Emerson Smith, *Colonists in Bondage: White Servitude and Convict Labor in America, 1607–1776* (Chapel Hill: University of North Carolina Press, 1947); and Sharon V. Salinger, *"To Serve Well and Faithfully": Labor and Indentured Servants in Pennsylvania, 1682–1800* (Cambridge: Cambridge University Press, 1987).

4. J. A. Leo Lemay and P. M. Zall, eds., *Benjamin Franklin's Autobiography: An Authoritative Text, Backgrounds, Criticism* (New York: Norton, 1986).

5. Accounts written by Moraley's contemporaries are listed in the Bibliography at the end of this Introduction.

Moraley's travels in North America form the central event in his autobiography, originally entitled *The Infortunate: or, the Voyage and Adventures of William Moraley, of Moraley, in the County of Northumberland, Gent{leman,}-From his Birth, to the Present Time. Containing Whatever is Curious and Remarkable in the Provinces of Pen{n}sylvania and New Jersey: an Account of the Laws and Customs of the Inhabitants; the Product, Soil and Climate; also the Author's Several Adventures though Divers Parts of America, and His Surprising Return to Newcastle. To Which is Added His Case, Recommended to the Gentlemen of the Law.* As the subtitle suggests, he designed the book both to inform and to entertain. He describes various exotic features of North America, both its land and its inhabitants, and narrates his life and escapades in the New World. He also includes three unrelated stories (in Chapters 2, 4, and 9), examples of the anecdotes he undoubtedly told to pass time on board ship, in a tavern, or to his customers while cleaning and repairing their clocks. The memoir concludes with a detailed justification for his behavior and his failures after returning to Newcastle upon Tyne, England.

The remainder of this Introduction provides information to help readers understand and interpret the memoir. It considers the characteristics of labor and migration in the world of William Moraley, the places he visited and the kinds of people he met, the transformation in the nature of families of which he was a part, the occupational groups to which he belonged, the intellectual developments that shaped his thinking, and the literary developments of the era within which he wrote the autobiography, as well as suggestions about how to approach the text.[6]

Labor and Migration

Like at least half of all European migrants to the British North American colonies during the eighteenth century, William Moraley signed a contract

6. Recent treatments of Moraley's memoir by scholars and teachers include the following: Billy G. Smith, "Walking Moraley's Streets: Philadelphia," *COMMON-PLACE*, 3:4 (July 2003), http://www .common-place.org/vol-03/no-04/philadelphia; Michael Zuckerman, "Tocqueville, Turner, and Turds: Four Stories of Manners in Early America," *Journal of American History* 85:1 (1998):13–42, and the responses in that issue; Farley Grubb, "Fatherless and Friendless: Factors Influencing the Flow of English Emigrant Servants," *Journal of Economic History* 52 (1992): 85–108; Kenneth Kusmer, *Down and Out and on the Road: The Homeless in American History* (New York: Oxford, 2001). A middle-school lesson plan based on the autobiography is in Marion Menzin, "How and Why They Came: Narratives of Migration," *OAH Magazine of History* 18 (April 2004): 38–42.

called an indenture. By this agreement, an immigrant worked as a servant
for between three and seven years for a designated master. In payment for
their work, servants received passage across the Atlantic, daily maintenance (including food, shelter, and clothing), and, if fortunate, "freedom
dues" at the conclusion of their term. Freedom dues in the seventeenth
century sometimes included land, but by the eighteenth century (when
Moraley arrived) former servants might be rewarded with a few clothes,
some tools, a little cash, or nothing at all. Slightly more than half of all
indentured servants in the eighteenth century were young men in late
adolescence, most of whom either were farmers or lacked any occupational
skills. Skilled artisans, like Moraley, usually were older when they signed
an indenture (Moraley was thirty), since they had been apprentices
through their teens.[7]

A brief period of peace on the high seas, famine in Ireland, war in Germany, and economic difficulties in England all encouraged William
Moraley and thousands of others to emigrate to the New World in the
late 1720s and the 1730s. Approximately 73,000 Europeans traveled to
British North America during the 1730s, nearly twice as many as the
average during each of the century's first three decades. With its temper-
ate climate, religious toleration, and generally expanding economy, the
Delaware River Valley was an attractive destination; at least 17,000
migrants arrived in Philadelphia's port in the 1730s.[8]

Scholars have long speculated about the various forces that impel people to uproot themselves, usually dividing these into "push" factors, which
compel individuals to leave their homes, or "pull" factors, which entice
them to another place. Push factors are often economic in nature,

---

7. Galenson, *White Servitude in Colonial America*; Smith, *Colonists in Bondage*; and Salinger, *"To Serve Well and Faithfully."*

8. The number of immigrants is drawn from Henry A. Gemery, "Disarray in the Historical Record: Estimates of Immigration to the United States, 1700–1860," in Susan E. Klepp, ed., *The Demographic History of the Philadelphia Region, 1600–1860* (Philadelphia: American Philosophical Society, 1989), 126, table 1; Klepp, "Demography in Early Philadelphia, 1690–1860," ibid., 111, table 4; Jean R. Soderlund, "Black Importation and Migration into Southeastern Pennsylvania, 1682–1810," ibid., 146, table 1; Wokeck, "German and Irish Immigration to Colonial Philadelphia," ibid., 128-43; and Darold W. Wax, "The Negro Slave Trade in Colonial Pennsylvania" (Ph.D. diss., University of Washington, 1962), 46, table 1, and 48, table 2. The changing character of the migrants is from Salinger, *"To Serve Well and Faithfully,"* 47–60, 178. For 1729, the year Moraley landed, there is an unusually detailed tally of arrivals at the port of Philadelphia: 267 English and Welsh passengers arrived, of whom 68 were indentured servants; 1,155 Irish passengers arrived, of whom 230 were servants; 43 servants from Scotland arrived; and 243 Palatines arrived as paying passengers. An additional 4,500 passengers, most of whom were from Ireland, landed in Delaware (John Oldmixon, *The British Empire in America* [London, 1741], 321).

although politics, war, religion, social nonconformity, alienation, a criminal record, indebtedness, and family difficulties can also be powerful factors in the decision to migrate. Pull factors are also frequently economic and can include access to land, employment opportunities, finding a haven from creditors or other persecution, or simple escape from personal problems. The plight of immigrants to the colonies was shifting during Moraley's stay in America. Poorer people were becoming a larger portion of the arrivals than had been the case earlier. By Moraley's time, the most valuable farms in southeastern Pennsylvania had been claimed, forcing the "poorer sort," according to historical geographer James T. Lemon, to move "beyond the limits of settlement and speculative holdings" if they hoped to obtain real estate.[9] Nearly one in three passengers disembarking at Philadelphia in the 1730s was an indentured servant, and they were joined by involuntary, enslaved men, women, and children from West Africa and the Caribbean. Migrants, especially those from England, tended to be young, aged sixteen to twenty-six, single, and male. There were eleven men for every woman among English emigrants to Pennsylvania between 1729 and 1734. Like Moraley, these young men were often fatherless and friendless.[10]

Places and Peoples

When Moraley left his native country in 1729, Great Britain was an aggressive nation struggling to exercise power over much of the Atlantic World. During the previous half century, Britain had increased its influence in North America, acquired profitable sugar colonies in the Caribbean, gained considerable control over the slave trade with Africa, and expanded commerce with India. Meanwhile, the process of nation building in the British Isles united nearly ten million people in England, Wales, and Scotland as citizens or, in the case of Ireland, as subjects of a centralized state. Literacy expanded and connected a national reading public

9. James T. Lemon, *The Best Poor Man's Country: A Geographical Study of Early Southeastern Pennsylvania* (New York: Norton, 1972), 68.

10. Statistics calculated from Galenson, *White Servitude in Colonial America*, 219–37. See also Aaron S. Fogleman, "From Slaves, Convicts, and Servants to Free Passengers: The Transformation of Immigration in the Era of the American Revolution," *Journal of American History* 85 (1998): 43–74; Grubb, "Fatherless and Friendless," 85–108.

through books, newspapers, magazines, and pamphlets. Reading was far from the only available pleasure. Comfort and fashion—clocks, furniture, tea, chocolate, silks, calicoes, and china—could be purchased by growing numbers of English men and women, and they demanded new products made at home or imported from abroad. London, with a population of 750,000 in the early eighteenth century, was the largest and most impressive city in Europe. It was dirty, unhealthy, and overcrowded, yet vibrant, exciting, and sophisticated. Newspapers, government offices, book publishers, print sellers, theaters, concerts, coffee shops, taverns, and the latest fashions vied for attention. Young people from all over the British Isles flocked to the metropolitan center of the empire out of desperation, a sense of adventure, or the quest for a better material life. Extremes of wealth and indigence were apparent everywhere: in housing, clothing, travel, education, occupation, and opportunity. A wealthy British aristocracy enjoyed considerable privileges based solely on their birthright, a growing group of merchants earned fabulous fortunes directing Atlantic World commerce, and, simultaneously, destitution was pervasive.[11]

When Moraley arrived in the Middle Colonies, Pennsylvania and New Jersey were still raw frontier settlements, with a combined population of less than ninety thousand people. Philadelphia was the largest town, with only about seven thousand inhabitants; its nearest rival (where Moraley initially lived) was Burlington, New Jersey, a village of a few hundred residents. Benjamin Franklin had just become editor of the *Pennsylvania Gazette*, and Philadelphia contained a few coffee shops and many taverns, but neither town provided the attractions of London. The vast majority of inhabitants lived in the country and farmed for a living. The politically powerful Penn family were aristocrats who enjoyed important feudal privileges, including the income from land sales and from quit-rents (annual taxes) on all real estate, but few others of the gentry classes lived in the Mid-Atlantic colonies. To a greater degree than in Britain, bound, unfree labor—slaves, convicts, indentured servants, and "redemptioners" (bound

11. Roy Porter, *English Society in the Eighteenth Century* (London: Penguin, 1982); Lorna Weatherill, *Consumer Behavior and Material Culture in Britain, 1660–1760* (London: Routledge, 1988); Dorothy George, *England in Transition: Life and Work in the Eighteenth Century* (Baltimore: Penguin, 1965 [1931]); Linda Colley, *Britons: Forging the Nation, 1707–1837* (New Haven: Yale University Press, 1992); Joyce Ellis, "The 'Black Indies:' The Economic Development of Newcastle, c. 1700–1840," in *Newcastle upon Tyne: A Modern History,* ed. Robert Calls and Bill Lancaster (London: Phillimore, 2001); Kathleen Wilson, *The Sense of the People: Politics, Culture, and Imperialism in England, 1715–1785* (New York: Cambridge University Press, 1995); John Brewer, *The Pleasures of the Imagination: English Culture in the Eighteenth Century* (Chicago: University of Chicago Press, 1997).

laborers who came without the contractual guarantees that most English servants had)—performed a great deal of the daily work by plowing, planting, weeding, and harvesting fields; carting and carrying goods; harnessing, driving, and feeding livestock; weaving, sewing, and washing clothes; building, sweeping, cleaning, and repairing structures; and manufacturing, by hand, many of the goods sold locally and abroad.[12]

The countryside in England was ethnically and religiously homogeneous, although Irish, Scottish, and foreign merchants and seamen lived in the larger towns like London and Newcastle. The Middle Colonies, however, were far more diverse. While Native Americans had ceded some territory to the new arrivals, the Lenape, Munsi, Shawnee, Susquehannocks, and other indigenous people continued to live in the region. Pennsylvania and New Jersey had previously absorbed Swedish, Finnish, and Dutch colonists along with migrants from all parts of the British Isles, while a rapidly growing German population joined a smattering of Swiss, French, and other European settlers. The demand for labor and the capital accumulation that accompanied Philadelphia's early economic growth stimulated the forced importation of hundreds of slaves during the 1720s. When Moraley arrived in Philadelphia, African and Caribbean people comprised approximately 15 percent of the urban residents, working as laborers along the wharves, mariners on ships, skilled workers in artisans' shops, and domestics in the homes of the affluent.[13]

Families

Families performed many more functions in the early eighteenth century than they do today. Most important, production was largely carried on within households, providing an economic component to nearly all familial relationships. Marriages, at least among those who possessed wealth or property, were calculated to maximize the material advantages to all concerned parties: the husband's interest came first, then the wife's, but both the husband's and the wife's natal families also expected benefits. Parents,

12. Gary B. Nash, *Quakers and Politics: Pennsylvania, 1681–1726* (Princeton: Princeton University Press, 1968, reprinted 1997); Smith, "Walking Moraley's Streets."

13. Joseph E. Illick, *Colonial Pennsylvania: A History* (New York: Charles Scribner's Sons, 1976); Billy G. Smith, "Benjamin Franklin: Civic Improver," in Richard R. Dunn and John C. Van Horne, eds., *Benjamin Franklin: In Search of a Better World* (New Haven: Yale University Press, forthcoming).

especially in rural areas, perceived children as a vital source of income, and they put them to work at a very young age. Apprentices, servants, and slaves were also expected to be productive, and household heads considered them as members of the family nearly on a par with the children. The father operated as head of the household, responsible for the welfare and discipline of its members, the education of children, and interactions with authorities outside the family. He served in the stead of the monarch, protecting and preserving social order.[14]

Wives were *femes covert*: their husbands "covered" their wives' identities, and women ceased to enjoy a separate legal existence once married. Women's dowries, wages, and other property, even their clothing, belonged to their husbands, as did their bodies, their labor, and their children. Women did share with their husbands the governance of children, servants, and slaves, and they were in charge of food, clothing, and health. Children were to be obedient to mothers but even more so to fathers, who controlled the patrimony of each child and could wield their power to great effect. Inheritance was much more of a determinant of social status than was the accumulation of wages over the course of a lifetime. Boys whose parents could not afford the fee for their apprenticeship to a well-paying occupation and girls without a substantial dowry often enjoyed few opportunities beyond servitude, dependence, financial struggle, and poverty.

In early eighteenth-century England, youths customarily spent their adolescence and early adulthood as either servants or apprentices. Marriage was discouraged until they gained their freedom, accumulated necessary household goods, learned the basic skills of their trade, and achieved the ability to support a family. For most English citizens, these requirements meant relatively late marriages; on average, women wed at age twenty-six and men at twenty-eight. Relatively rare, and much criticized, were people who undertook familial responsibilities before realizing economic and social independence. Celibacy and dependency characterized the expected condition of young men and women, and at least one of every nine of Moraley's adult peers never gained sufficient autonomy to wed. In

14. For information about families in Britain and America in this and the following paragraphs, see John R. Gillis, *For Better, For Worse: British Marriages, 1600 to the Present* (New York: Oxford University Press, 1985); Lawrence Stone, *The Family, Sex, and Marriage in England, 1500–1800* (New York: Harper & Row, 1977); Steven Mintz and Susan Kellogg, *Domestic Revolutions: A Social History of American Family Life* (New York: The Free Press, 1988); Laurel Thatcher Ulrich, *Good Wives: Image and Reality in the Lives of Women in Northern New England* (New York: Oxford University Press, 1983); J. William Frost, *The Quaker Family in Colonial America* (New York: St. Martin's, 1973); and Barry Levy, *Quakers and the American Family: British Settlement in the Delaware Valley* (New York: Oxford University Press, 1988).

the colonies, many bound white workers could not marry by the terms of their indenture. For the free population in British North America, however, easier access to land usually allowed marriages at younger ages than in England.

During Moraley's lifetime, the perception and functions of the family changed rapidly. Emotional considerations began to supersede (although not eliminate) economic issues. Romantic love, or at least companionship, increasingly became the primary reason for marriage. Ideally, men should avoid raw expressions of patriarchal authority. Novels and magazines advocated that sympathy, sensibility, and other generous emotions should be cultivated in the home. Husbands and wives should complement one another. Husbands should be primarily concerned about their wives' well-being, while wives willingly (not forcibly) obeyed their husbands out of recognition of their kindly and well-meaning direction. Parents should love and cherish their children rather than exploit or discipline them harshly. Among the upper classes in particular, indulgent fathers and mothers valued the individuality of their offspring within a sentimental, loving relationship; they replaced authoritarian parents who rigidly enforced obedience and dependence in their children. Apprentices, servants, and slaves grew increasingly distant from this newly intimate circle of affectionate parents and children. The distinct differences between these two systems of marriage and parenting created tensions throughout the eighteenth and nineteenth centuries and provide a major theme and source of conflict in Moraley's life as well.

Legal Profession

William Moraley was fifteen years old in 1714, when his father bound him as a clerk to an attorney. This was an expensive undertaking; his father probably paid the lawyer between £150 and £200 to take his son as a clerk and teach him the law. However, success in that profession required more than just money. The "Professor of this Science," according to a contemporary career handbook, "must not be born a Blockhead; he must have a clear solid, unclouded Understanding, a distinguishing Head, and a puzzling, unpuzzled Brain." In addition, the clerk should be a "Gentleman born" (which Moraley, the son of a watchmaker, certainly was not) and liberally educated. Moraley had been provided with a pedigree and had studied—if in a lackadaisical fashion—Latin, history, theology, arithmetic, and science. However, because he did not come from the upper classes, Moraley may not have felt comfortable in the world of lawyers, which may partially explain why he did not apply himself or succeed as an attorney.[15]

Technically, a law clerk was a journeyman who earned a maximum wage of ten shillings and six pence per week—an insubstantial income given the expense of living in London and behaving like a gentleman. Modest wages and high expectations caused many clerks to fall into debt. The combination of lightly supervised adolescent clerks, a genteel ethos, and considerable financial pressure sometimes resulted, according to the career guide, in "Cheating, Lewdness, and all manner of Debachery [Debauchery] being often more studied than Law or Precedents."[16]

Given the reputation of law clerks and the substantial investment in Moraley's clerkship, it is surprising that his father discovered only belatedly, in 1718, that he did not approve of the legal profession as a career for his son. One ungenerous interpretation is that the father withdrew his support from his son at a time when he was investing heavily in the South Sea Company. The £800 that the father eventually lost in the crash of the stock was close to the average of £1,000 needed to purchase chambers (offices) for a new attorney. Young William's change in status from a lawyer's clerk to a watchmaker's apprentice was substantial. In one stroke of the pen at the Guildhall, the nineteen-year-old went from a promising profession to a common trade, from journeyman to apprentice, from independence to daily subservience to his father. That the South Sea Bubble burst two years later only added to his misfortune by depleting the family's wealth.[17]

15. R. Campbell, *The London Tradesman* . . . (1747; reprint, Devon: David & Charles, 1969), quotations from 70, 71, 331. Of the 145 young men articled to attorneys in 1714, 20 percent came from a middling background, 56 percent hailed from the gentry, and 6 percent were from the "poorer sort"; the origins of the balance were uncertain but probably from genteel circumstances (calculated from Michael Miles, "'A Haven for the Privileged': Recruitment into the Profession of Attorney in England, 1709–1792," *Social History* 11 [1986]: 197–210).

16. Campbell, *London Tradesman*, 72–73.

17. Ibid., 331. On May 5, 1718, William Moraley (spelled Morley) was bound as an apprentice to his father for the very small sum of 2 shillings and 6 pence; £20 was the customary fee for clockmakers' apprenticeship. Moraley's apprenticeship is in the Clockmakers Company, Court Minutes, Volume 3, Ms 2710/3, Guildhall Library and Manuscripts, London. Keith Bates notes the customary fee in *The Clockmakers of Northumberland and Durham* (Rohbury, Morpeth, Northumberland: Pendulum Publications, 1980), 13. Moraley and his father may have considered that the apparent surplus of attorneys would make a £1,000 investment in a fledgling law practice riskier than putting the money in South Sea Company stock. Between 1712 and the market crash of 1720, some 119 new law clerks were registered each year. For the

British Artisans and Markets

The primarily male artisanal world in which Moraley operated after the end of his legal clerkship consisted of three tiers: apprentices, journeymen, and masters. Ideally, artisans made steady progress during their careers, moving from apprentice to journeyman to master of their craft. A young adolescent usually served for between four and ten years as an apprentice, and, in return for his unpaid labor, he received instruction in basic skills, daily maintenance, and often a small gift of clothes or tools from his master at the end of the apprenticeship. A journeyman hired out for wages to a master, but generally owned his own tools. He might labor for a number of years in that status, working for various masters, waiting to accumulate both the capital and the additional skills necessary to establish himself as a master. Where guilds existed, a journeyman needed to produce a master piece of work, proof of his command of the skills of his craft, and be voted into the guild in order to practice his trade. Only a master craftsman was independent, typically working for himself out of his home. He was free to marry, establish his own household and shop, and hire journeymen and take on apprentices as assistants.[18]

This ideal career, however, frequently did not match reality. Besides learning the required skills, one of the greatest obstacles was gaining access to the capital necessary for a journeyman to set up as an independent master. Even in William Hogarth's rendering of the supremely successful career (see Figs. 1, 2, and 3), hard work and thrift did not bring a slow and steady accumulation of capital. Instead, hard work gained the industrious apprentice a good reputation, and his reward was the hand of his master's daughter and partnership in an established enterprise. Rather than earning independence in his own right, the fortunate apprentice would be endowed with capital by his social superiors through familial channels. Thus, many journeymen remained wage earners for their entire lives no matter how hard they labored and tried to save.

The art of watchmaking was, as the great economist Adam Smith observed, "much superior to common trades."[19] A master clockmaker or

---

remainder of the century, the annual average was less that half that number (calculated from Miles, "'A Haven for the Privileged,'" 199, table 1).

18. Ronald Schultz, *The Republic of Labor: Philadelphia Artisans and the Politics of Class, 1720–1830* (New York: Oxford University Press, 1993).

19. Adam Smith, *An Inquiry into the Nature and Causes of the Wealth of Nations*, 2 vols., ed. James E. Thorold Rogers (Oxford: Clarendon Press, 1869), 1:129.

watchmaker had to understand metallurgy, the mechanics of wheels, pulleys, and springs, and the related crafts of silver- and goldsmiths, cabinetmakers, jewelers, engravers, enamelers, glaziers, and chainmakers. He also needed some comprehension of the physics of motion.[20] The apprentice should therefore possess "a Mechanic Head, [and] a light nice Hand," according to the career handbook, but "no great Strength, nor much Education" was necessary.[21] Access to the trade was more difficult than for most crafts. Apprenticeship fees ranged from £10 to £30, placing watchmaking among the most expensive 20 percent of occupations for entrance costs.[22] In London, the Clockmakers Company severely limited the number of available apprenticeships as a means to curtail competition.[23]

Between 1660 and 1775, London's supremacy in clockmaking and watchmaking was unchallenged at home or abroad. After about 1670, mass production of watches became possible because of the introduction of standardized parts, an elaborate division of labor, and the subcontracting of tasks to less-skilled workers in garrets and individual households. Watchmakers were also innovative retailers, moving their fragile products from open stalls to shops with glass cases, large windows, and comfortable chairs for customers. To rent a workshop and to purchase essential tools and raw materials cost between £50 and £100. However, it took months to develop a client base and even more time for customers to pay for the goods. The £300 that Moraley expected to inherit from his father would have enabled him to become independent, but the £20 that his mother eventually gave him was far too little.[24]

---

20. M. Dorothy George, *London Life in the Eighteenth Century* (New York: Capricorn, 1965), 176; G. H. Baillie, C. Clutton, and C. A. Ilbert, *Britten's Old Clocks and Watches and Their Makers* (New York: Dutton, 1956), 270.

21. Campbell, *London Tradesman*, 252.

22. Apprenticeship fees charged by watchmakers and clockmakers, at £30 maximum, ranked above the average range of £10 to £20 for the 323 occupations listed in Campbell, *London Tradesman*, 331–40. Watch finishers could command up to £20 for an apprentice, and watch-movement-makers as much as £10, although chainmakers—a cottage industry dominated by women workers—required no apprentice fees. Lawyers charged £200 to take on a clerk, and positions with merchants and bankers cost even more. Among the lines of employment that did not necessitate an entrance fee, a few, such as physicians, required university training, but most were lesser skilled occupations. The distribution of apprenticeship fees for the 323 occupations are as follows: 27 percent cost £5 or less; 28 percent cost between £5 and £10; 28 percent cost between £10 and £20; and 17 percent cost more than £20.

23. George, *London Life*, 176; Baillie, Clutton, and Ilbert, *Britten's Old Clocks*, 270.

24. William Petty, "Another Essay in Political Arithmetick, Concerning the Growth of the City of London (1683)," in Charles Henry Hull, ed., *The Economic Writings of Sir William Petty*, 2 vols. (New York: Kelley, 1964), 2:473; E. J. Tyler, *The Craft of the Clockmaker* (London: Ward, Lock, 1973), 24–25, 62; David S. Landes, *Revolution in Time: Clocks and the Making of the Modern World* (Cambridge, Mass.: Belknap Press of Harvard University Press, 1983), 219–36.

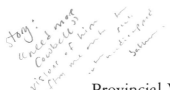

Provincial Watchmakers and Markets

Clockmakers and watchmakers outside London could not compete with the city's more highly skilled artisans. In the English countryside, most clockmakers sold London-made watches, created tall clocks, and repaired their customers' timepieces. Few clockmakers' companies or guilds existed outside the capital, and none was in either Newcastle or the colonies; thus, technically, anyone might enter the trade, thereby increasing competition and lowering profits and wages.[25] In the colonies, the conditions of clockmakers and watchmakers were even less organized and more primitive than in the English countryside. Rural watchmakers rarely specialized in a single craft. Moraley's owner, Isaac Pearson, for example, was a master clockmaker who had apprenticed in Philadelphia, but who also worked as a farmer, silversmith, goldsmith, blacksmith, and buttonmaker. He received additional income from his political and civic activities and from his investments in real estate and the iron forge at Mount Holly.

One result of the lack of specialization in the colonies was that local clocks were inferior to English standards of craftsmanship. One of the still-extant clocks from Isaac Pearson's workshop, for instance, has "the appearance of English workmanship" and is "nicely proportioned and pleasing to the eye." However, as one expert points out, the engraved inscription, "TEMPUS FUGIT" (Latin for "time flies"), was misspelled as "TEPUS FUG IT," with the missing "M" scratched in later above the "P." Moreover, the internal mechanisms of this clock employ wrought iron where brass should have been used, the plates are of varying thicknesses, and the copper is soft from being insufficiently worked. Imported clocks and watches were of much higher quality.[26]

The small, scattered population dotting the Delaware Valley owned relatively few timepieces during the early eighteenth century, creating small demand for the services of clockmakers like Moraley, and perhaps explaining why he was sold last among the boatload of indentured servants with

25. George, *London Life*, 176; Baillie, Clutton, and Ilbert, *Britten's Old Clocks*, 270–72.

26. Seven clocks from the workshop of Isaac Pearson have survived. Only one is dated, and none indicates the names of journeymen or apprentices. The Decorative Arts Catalogue in the Winterthur Museum (Delaware) describes the clocks. Charles J. Burton, "A New Jersey Clock," *Bulletin of the National Association of Watch and Clock Collectors* 8 (1958): quotes on 213–14. The clock in Figure 14 is tentatively dated to 1735, about the time of Moraley's indenture. See also Carl M. Williams, *Silversmiths of New Jersey, 1700–1825, with Some Notice of Clockmakers who Were Also Silversmiths* (Philadelphia: George S. McManus, 1949), 34–44.

whom he arrived. Affluent residents invested more in land and labor than in consumer goods. Perhaps only one of every twenty rural householders owned a timepiece, and even in Philadelphia "only men in easy circumstances carried a watch," often a London import. By contrast, 30 percent of English rural households and 50 percent of London households had a clock or watch.[27] Since a relatively large number of clockmakers lived in the Delaware Valley, the competition for the market was stiff and employment possibilities limited.[28] Not for another generation would the region's clock and watchmakers be able to fashion a more fully developed industry along English lines.[29] Like so many indentured servants, Moraley's timing in moving to the colonies was less than ideal.

27. An analysis of inventories of estates in southeastern Pennsylvania and northern Delaware between 1690 and 1735 found that only 5 percent of rural households and 25 percent of Philadelphia households owned a clock. Just 17 percent of the inventories listed any timepieces in Hunterdon and Burlington counties in New Jersey during the first half of the century, few of which were watches. See Jack Michel, " 'In a Manner and Fashion Suitable to Their Degree': A Preliminary Investigation of the Material Culture of Early Rural Pennsylvania" (paper presented to the Philadelphia Center for Early American Studies, 1981), 7, 75, 81; and Weatherill, *Consumer Behavior and Material Culture in Britain,* 27, table 2.2, and 89, table 4.4. See also Joan Jensen, *Loosening the Bonds: Mid-Atlantic Farm Women, 1750–1800* (New Haven: Yale University Press, 1986), 55. Information on New Jersey inventories, 1714–44 and 1759–89, is derived from samples collected by Judy A. McGaw as part of her continuing research project. Two-thirds of the timepieces inventoried in Burlington and Hunterdon counties in the first half of the century were clocks; watches did not become common until the century's second half. Studies of inventories from rural Massachusetts and rural Maryland also found that very few households owned timepieces before mid-century. See Gloria L. Main, "The Standard of Living in Southern New England, 1640–1773," *William and Mary Quarterly,* 3rd ser., 45 (January 1988): 134; and Lois Green Carr and Lorena S. Walsh, "The Standard of Living in the Colonial Chesapeake," ibid., 146. Quotation from John F. Watson, *Annals of Philadelphia, and Pennsylvania, in the Olden Time,* 3 vols. (Philadelphia: Stuart, 1899), 1:218.

28. Moraley mentions four clockmakers in Philadelphia, two of whom quickly decided to try their luck elsewhere. Peter Stretch was the "eminent" clockmaker who dominated the profession in the city. Arriving in 1702 at the age of thirty-two, Stretch produced dozens of tall-case clocks, which provided refinement to the homes of the affluent. Stretch was also prominent politically and religiously, serving for thirty-eight years as a city councilman and participating in Quaker affairs. However, where Stretch succeeded materially and socially, Moraley would fail. Moraley also indicates that he cleaned and repaired two timepieces in one day. If this were a normal workday, then four craftsmen, working the standard six-day week, could easily clean and repair 2,500 timepieces annually without the assistance of apprentices or journeymen. Yet, as Jack Michel suggests, there were only 350 clocks in the city, so it is doubtful that there was sufficient employment for four watchmakers and clockmakers. See Michel, " 'In a Manner and Fashion Suitable to Their Degree' "; and Edward E. Chandlee, *Six Quaker Clockmakers* (Philadelphia: Historical Society of Pennsylvania, 1943). Pennsylvania was the center of the American trade, however, a factor that might have served to attract artisans. From the founding of the colonies until 1825, some 194 clockmakers are known to have worked in Pennsylvania, by far the largest number in any colony or state and more than one-fourth of all the clockmakers who operated in British North America. D. W. Hering, "Geographical Distribution of Early Clockmaking in America," *American Collector* 6, no. 10 (1937): 23.

29. Finding sufficient manufacturing and repair work in the face of a saturated market remained a problem for watchmakers and clockmakers into the nineteenth century; see Philip Zea, "Clockmaking and Society at the River and the Bay: Jedidiah and Jabez Baldwin, 1790–1820," in Peter Benes, ed., *The Dublin Seminar for New England Folklife, Annual Proceedings, 1981: The Bay and the River, 1600–1900* (Boston:

Religion and Enlightenment

The active promotion of immigration and the tolerant religious policies of Pennsylvania and New Jersey encouraged a greater medley of faiths and practices in the Mid-Atlantic region than anywhere in Europe or even in other colonies. Unlike in most of the Western world, there was no established church, no church courts, no required attendance at worship services, and no mandatory tithing to support a government-approved faith. The region's Quakers and other pietists promoted freedom of individual conscience, while many Anglicans were latitudinarians: they embraced a rational, loving religion that provided followers wide discretion in both belief and ritual. Anglicans, Quakers, Presbyterians, Lutherans, Reformed (German Calvinists), Baptists, Moravians, Schwenkfelders, Mennonites, Seventh-day Brethren, Rosecrucians, Catholics, Jews, and others coexisted in relative harmony in Pennsylvania and New Jersey.

This state of affairs astonished many European visitors who remembered their own vicious religious wars of the previous century, although some visiting clerics worried about the considerable number of people who practiced no religion at all. Some radical religious groups experimented with communal living and childrearing, gender equality, abolition of the priesthood, pacifism, antislavery activism, celibacy, or the denial of the existence of sin, raising anxieties among some outside observers about the presence of evil and social disorder. Moraley's arrival in America coincided with the beginnings of the Great Awakening, a religious revival characterized by a belief in the possibility of universal salvation, human equality in the eyes of God, and an emphasis on the heart rather than on reason. Many churches split in consequence of the turmoil of the 1730s and the following decades. Yet, toleration for a certain level of disagreement and contention, innovation, charity, education, and an emphasis on both rationality and emotion continued to characterize many of the faiths present in the Delaware Valley.[30]

Various philosophical trends in the late seventeenth and eighteenth cen-

---

Boston University Press, 1982), 43–59. Nearly all studies of clockmaking in the eighteenth-century Delaware Valley focus on its technological aspects rather than on the economic development of the craft, but see Frank D. Prager, ed., *The Autobiography of John Fitch* (Philadelphia: American Philosophical Society, 1976); and Alfred Coxe Prime, *The Arts and Crafts in Philadelphia, Maryland, and South Carolina*, 2 vols. (1929; reprint, New York: Da Capo Press, 1969), 1:225–73, 2:238–73.

30. Sally Schwartz, *"A Mixed Multitude": The Struggle for Toleration in Colonial Pennsylvania* (New York: New York University Press, 1988); J. William Frost, *A Perfect Freedom: Religious Liberty in Pennsylvania* (New York: Cambridge University Press, 1990).

turies contributed to the intellectual movement known as the Enlightenment. Inspired in part by the theories of Sir Isaac Newton and John Locke and popularized by novelists, playwrights, and pamphleteers, Enlightenment thinkers advocated scientific investigation, rationality, order, universal physical laws, and the essential beneficence of nature. They applied these methods and assumptions to the leading questions of the day. What was the nature of the universe? How can seemingly random events like weather, epidemics, or historical change be understood? How can the existence and intensions of God be detected in His creation? What is human nature? What is the basis of politics? Is royalty necessary? Are there natural rights? What is liberty, justice, and, especially, virtue? Can the oppression of the poor, the insane, the criminal, the enslaved, and women ever be justified? Are social hierarchies necessary? Are prisons required? Can there be progress? There was little agreement about the answers to these questions, but the debate itself undermined older assumptions of unquestioning faith in traditional authorities.[31]

Enlightened discourse favored curiosity, a confidence in human intellectual capacity, a distrust of arguments based solely on claims of authority, a focus on new and fresh approaches, and an expectation of practical results. These tendencies affected not only the learned but also those who only perused an annual almanac or who heard others reading out loud from newspapers and books. Many artisans and common folk, including William Moraley and Benjamin Franklin, were inspired to join the public dialogue on these and many other issues.[32]

Reading and Writing

Contemporary literature helped shape Moraley's interpretation of his life, and it is only natural that his memoir was influenced by the literary styles of his time; they provided the organizational models a fledgling author required. Like most eighteenth-century authors, Moraley probably had to

31. There is a large literature on philosophical and religious ideas in the eighteenth century. Two places to begin are Ned Landsman, *From Colonials to Provincials: American Thought and Culture, 1680–1760* (Ithaca: Cornell University Press, 2000), and Patricia Bonomi, *Under the Cope of Heaven: Religion, Society, and Politics in Colonial America* (New York: Oxford University Press, 2003). See also Henry F. May, *The Enlightenment in America* (New York: Oxford University Press, 1976).

32. Landsman, *From Colonials to Provincials*.

pay his printer (John White, who published the local newspaper, the *New-castle Courant*) in advance. Since Moraley was struggling financially, he undoubtedly kept in mind the preferences of his potential audience while he wrote; nothing but a large sale would repay his investment, especially since the one-shilling cost of the book was modest. Only six copies of the original are known to have survived, an indication both of a small press run and that few copies actually sold. By the nineteenth century, *The Infortunate* was already considered an extremely rare book.[33]

Overall, the text bears some resemblance to contemporary magazines in its mixture of fact and fiction, prose and poetry, love stories and a murder, animal lore and governmental policy, simple description and his own very personal adventures. In depicting himself as a "picaresque" hero, Moraley wrote in a well-established genre stretching from sixteenth-century Spanish writers to Elizabethan authors to such eighteenth-century novelists as Daniel Defoe and Jonathan Swift. In their real or fictive journeys from place to place, picaros sought adventures that would contribute both to their increasing awareness of the world and to their maturity. One primary purpose of these stories was to entertain. Using this approach, Moraley diverted readers with tales not only about himself and his observations but also about other people's exotic travels and their dangerous and thrilling escapades.[34]

Personal accounts of travel, both nonfictional and fictional, enjoyed immense popularity in eighteenth-century England. William Dampier's *New Voyage Round the World of 1697*, Captain Cook's *Voyages,* and John Green's *New General Collection of Voyages and Travels, the World Display'd* were three best-sellers credited with reviving travel literature. An important component of this genre was its emphasis on the physical voyage through sometimes "bizarre" regions of the world as constituting a vital spiritual journey as well. The education gained through daily experience aided the evolution of the protagonist's moral consciousness. Of equal relevance are the novels of Daniel Defoe, especially *Robinson Crusoe,* a work

33. The publication of Moraley's book was advertised in the *Newcastle Courant*, July 16-23, 1743. See also John Philipson, "William Moraley, Watchmaker, of Newcastle (1699-1762)," *Archaeologia Aeliana; or, Miscellaneous Tracts Relating to Antiquity* (1993): 235-239.

34. See Raymond Hedrin, "The American Slave Narrative: The Justification of the Picaro," *American Literature* 53 (1982): 630–45; Henry Louis Gates Jr., "Binary Oppositions in Chapter One of *Narrative of the Life of Frederick Douglass, an American Slave, Written by Himself*," in *Afro-American Literature: The Reconstruction of Instruction*, ed. Dexter Fisher and Robert B. Stepto (New York: Modern Language Association of America, 1978), 214.

that undoubtedly influenced Moraley, since at one point he compared himself to its hero.[35]

Moraley's memoir also can be understood as part of the evolution of the autobiographical form. The religious introspection that characterized the seventeenth century, especially as fostered by such sects as the Puritans and the Quakers, produced a number of diaries and personal histories that looked inward at their state of faith and outward to detect signs of God's favors and punishments. Some religious authors wrote of their fall from grace and their struggles for redemption and salvation. The formula provided models that others might emulate. English autobiographies became increasingly secular during the eighteenth century. Personal success, defined in material terms or as service to humankind, replaced salvation as the goal, but struggle and triumph over enemies and adversity remained part of the story.[36]

The new genre of the novel likewise focused on the adversities facing the unwary hero or heroine. Novels, like autobiographies, plotted a meaningful trajectory in the recounting of adventures and personal development. Readers were interested not only in the lives of the rich and famous, but by the dispossessed and humbled as well. A considerable number of these novels (and a few plays) concerned "unfortunates": *The Unfortunate Traveller* (1594), *The Unfortunate Happy Lady* (ca. 1685), *Female Falsehood: or the Unfortunate Beau* (1697), *The Unfortunate Bride* (1700), *The Unfortunate Dutchess of Malfi* (1708), *The Mercenary Lover, or the Unfortunate Heiresses* (1726), *The Unfortunate Dutchess, or the Lucky Gamester* (1739), to note only a few published before Moraley wrote his account. Yet, even though the form of autobiographies and novels developed contemporaneously and in a similar fashion, autobiographies did not necessarily contain fictionalized passages. Authors of autobiographies might be selective, but they thought their real-life stories important and significant even before picking up their pens.

---

35. Peter N. Skrine, *The Baroque: Literature and Culture in Seventeenth-Century Europe* (New York: Holmes & Meier, 1978), 70–71; Angelo Costanzo, *Surprizing Narrative: Olaudah Equiano and the Beginnings of Black Autobiography* (New York: Greenwood Press, 1987), 48–49; Monroe Z. Hafter, "Toward a History of Spanish Imaginary Voyages," *Eighteenth-Century Studies* 8 (Spring 1975): 265–82; and Martin Green, *The Robinson Crusoe Story* (University Park: The Pennsylvania State University Press, 1990), chap 2.

36. On the parallel development of novels and autobiographies, see Wayne Shumaker, *English Autobiography: Its Emergence, Materials, and Form* (Berkeley and Los Angeles: University of California Press, 1954), 5, 20–30; Margaret Bottrall, *Every Man a Phoenix: Studies in Seventeenth-Century Autobiography* (London: William Clowes & Sons, 1958), 4, 141–44, 161–62; and Costanzo, *Surprising Narrative*, 49–51.

Approaches to the Text

Moraley's autobiography not only conveys an interesting story but also contains much of historical value. We have reproduced it with very few changes in order to allow Moraley to speak with his own voice. Chapter headings designed for a nineteenth-century reprinting have been included and slightly expanded for ease of reading and reference, a few typographical errors have been silently corrected, and the use of the British pound sign (£) has been modernized. Otherwise, spelling, punctuation, capitalization, grammar, and emphasis are as they appeared in the original 1743 version.[37]

Michel Eyguem de Montaigne, a prominent Renaissance philosopher, complained that historians too often spoil history because "they chew our meat for us." Scholarly analysis does not necessarily taint the taste of history, but nonspecialists can learn a great deal by chewing primary sources (like Moraley's memoir) for themselves. The Afterword in this volume sets the table with a discussion of the context of William Moraley's life. However, we encourage people to read the memoir first, so that they might enjoy the tale and act as historians in their own right by developing their interpretations, engaging in an intellectual adventure, and tasting more fully the rich and varied flavors of the past. To aid in that process of savoring the textures of the past, we suggest that readers consider the following issues and questions while discovering other insights and queries about William Moraley and the world of early America, Britain, and the Atlantic World.

Society and Labor

- Why does Moraley spend so much time delineating his ancestry?
- What were some of the causes of indigence and poverty in the eigh-

37. Abbreviated versions of Moraley's autobiography were published in the 1880s in the *Newcastle Weekly Chronicle* and the *Delaware County Republican*. Bound clippings from the latter source are available at the Historical Society of Pennsylvania and the New York Public Library. We have reprinted the complete and original version of the memoir available at the William L. Clements Library, University of Michigan, Ann Arbor. Excerpts are also available in the following: Kirsten Fischer and Eric Hinderaker, eds., *Colonial American History* (New York: Blackwell, 2002); Wayne Franklin, ed., *American Voices, American Lives: A Documentary Reader* (New York: Norton, 2001); Howard P. Chudacoff and Thomas G. Paterson, eds., *Major Problems in American Urban and Suburban History* (Boston: Houghton Mifflin, 2005); and History Matters,

teenth century? Were persons who worked hard guaranteed material success?

- Benjamin Franklin, a contemporary who may even have met Moraley in Burlington or Philadelphia, lived and popularized the rags-to-riches story that has been defined as quintessentially American. Franklin proposed thirteen secular "virtues" as the keys to success for the emerging middle class: temperance, silence, order, resolution, frugality, industry, sincerity, justice, moderation, cleanliness, tranquillity, chastity, and humility. What virtues do Moraley and his companions promote in their lives?
- Why might Moraley be considered more "traditional" and Franklin more "modern" in their views about life?
- What is the "American Dream?" Judging from Moraley's account, was it achieved commonly or rarely in his day?
- What are the roles of personality, education, social status, and economic conditions in achieving upward (or downward) mobility in Moraley's world?
- What other measures of success exist in Moraley's world besides wealth?
- What economic and social functions does the system of indentured servitude serve? To what extent does it benefit masters, servants, recruiters, ship captains, taxpayers, and/or government officials? To what extent is it exploitative?
- Does Moraley benefit from, or is he primarily a victim of, his experience as an indentured servant?

Class

- Historians often quote Moraley's comment that the Mid-Atlantic was "the best poor Man's County in the World" (53) as an accurate depiction of conditions in the British colonies. What evidence from Moraley's memoir supports or challenges this assertion?
- Where does Moraley seem to "fit" in the class structure of Britain and the Middle Colonies?

---

http://historymatters.gmu.edu/d/6229/. See Appendix A for more about the autobiography's publication history.

- How do issues associated with class shape Moraley's life and perspectives?
- What is the nature of the class structure of the American colonies? What are the roles and characteristics of different social groups?
- Who wields power in early North America, and how is it exercised? How much opportunity exists for the middle classes? For the poor? How about for African Americans, Native Americans, and women?
- Scholars sometimes characterize early America as a "deferential society." Did Moraley and his friends defer to their perceived "betters," or did they perceive themselves as equals or even as superiors? Were they obedient, impudent, subversive, rebellious, cooperative, or collegial in their relationships with their masters?

Migration and the Atlantic World

- Why does Moraley migrate to North America? Why does he return to England?
- The great majority of people who moved to North America in the eighteenth century were either slaves from Africa and the Caribbean or indentured servants from Europe, like Moraley. How would their migration likely shape colonial societies?
- What are the similarities and differences in the social and economic conditions between Britain and its colonies as suggested by Moraley's memoir?
- What does Moraley find appealing about Pennsylvania and New Jersey and why? What does he miss about England? What does he dislike about America? How different are the colonies compared to the mother country? Is America "exceptional"?

Worldview

- Why does Moraley believe in ghosts but not in witches?
- How important is religion to Moraley and to other eighteenth-century Americans?

- Based on the memoir, speculate about the prevalence of beliefs in fate, fortune, the stars (astrology), and other non-Christian ideas and the functions they serve.
- Do Quaker beliefs and practices influence Moraley's thinking?
- To what degree do scientific, rational, and "enlightened" ideas shape the views of Moraley and other people in the eighteenth century?
- Is there conflict between religion and science in Moraley's mind?
- What are Moraley's views of nature? Does he perceive American flora and fauna as resources to be exploited, as objects of scientific investigation, as exotic and alien curiosities, as proof of a divine plan, or as representative of an interconnected, interdependent ecological world?
- What are Moraley's views of government, the law, and politics?

Gender and Race

- How does Moraley view women? Why are there so few women in his account?
- In twenty-first-century America, social relationships are largely heterosocial—men and women work and socialize with members of the opposite sex. What types of relationships characterize Moraley's life? Why?
- What are Moraley's views of masculinity?
- How does Moraley compare his circumstances to that of slaves? What seems to be the relationship between indentured servitude and slavery? What different consequences seem to arise from humans selling their labor as opposed to being sold as property?
- How does Moraley depict Native Americans? By contrast, how does he perceive the condition of slaves? Can you tell what racial attitudes or stereotypes exist in the colonies that he may have adopted?

Social Conventions

- What does Moraley find amusing and why? Which of his acquaintances, superiors, or inferiors are the butts of jokes and tricks, and what purposes do these serve?

- What is the function of alcohol in Moraley's world?
- Moraley and his friends sometimes pilfer items. Under what circumstances do they justify taking other people's property?
- Clothing is important to Moraley. What does he find stylish, what is embarrassing or demeaning? How does clothing seem to reflect social status in his account?

The Memoir as Historical Document

- Why did Moraley write this book?
- What biases might readers anticipate when reading Moraley's account?
- If Moraley sometimes exaggerates wildly, then how can we trust the accuracy of other parts of his memoir?
- How useful is the memoir as historical evidence?
- Moraley includes three stories in his memoir: Sir George Sonds's two sons, The Fortunate Andalousian, and the Valentian: or Faithful Lover. Why might Moraley have chosen these particular stories to insert into his own account? What are the main themes of these stories and what meaning might the stories have had for him and his understanding of his own life?

Further Research

- Moraley's memoir can be compared to contemporary fictional accounts, especially the novels of Daniel Defoe, including *Robinson Crusoe* (1719) and *The Fortunes and Misfortunes of the Famous Moll Flanders* (1722), both available in many editions. See also Aphra Behn, *Oroonoko; or, the Royal Slave* (1696), and Joseph Addison, *Cato: A Tragedy* (1713). A useful guide to online reproductions of contemporary literature is "Eighteenth-Century E-Texts," by Jack Lynch of Rutgers University, http://andromeda.rutgers.edu/~jlynch/18th/.
- William Moraley's autobiography can also be compared to other first-hand accounts: Benjamin Franklin, Elizabeth Ashbridge, Olaudah Equiano, John Frederick Whitehead, William Apess, John Woolman, and other early Americans (see list below).

Contemporary Autobiographical Accounts

Alsop, George (1636?–1673?). *Character of the Province of Maryland* (1666), available at several sites online.

Apess, William (1798–1839). *A Son of the Forest* (1831, and many subsequent editions).

Ashbridge, Elizabeth Sampson (1713–1755). Daniel B. Shea, ed., "Some Account of the Fore Part of the Life of Elizabeth Ashbridge," in *Journeys in New Worlds: Early American Women's Narratives*, ed. William L. Andrews et al. (Madison: University of Wisconsin Press, 1990), 117–80.

Biddle, Charles (1745–1821). James S. Biddle, ed., *Autobiography of Charles Biddle, Vice-President of the Supreme Executive Council of Pennsylvania, 1745–1821* (privately printed) (Philadelphia: Claxton, 1883).

Buccau, Quamino, also Brocaw (1762–1850). William J. Allinson, *Memoir of Quamino Buccau, A Pious Methodist* (Philadelphia: Longstreth, 1851). Available online.

Cooper, Mary (1714–1778). *The Diary of Mary Cooper: Life on a Long Island Farm, 1768–1773*, ed. Field Horne (Oyster Bay, N.Y.: Oyster Bay Historical Society, 1981).

Dickewamis, also known as Mary Jemison (1742–1833). James E. Seaver, transcriber, *A Narrative of the Life of Mrs. Mary Jemison* (Syracuse: Syracuse University Press, 1990).

Equiano, Olaudah (1745–1797), also known as Gustavas Vassa or Jacob. *The Interesting Life of Olaudah Equiano or Gustavus Vassa, the African,* various editions.

Evans, David (1681–1750). Portions of his autobiography are printed in Boyd Stanley Schlenther, "'The English Is Swallowing up Their Language': Welsh Ethnic Ambivalence in Colonial Pennsylvania and the Experience of David Evans," *PMHB* 114 (1990): 201–28.

Fitch, John (1744–1798). *The Autobiography of John Fitch,* ed. Frank D. Prager (Philadelphia: APS, 1976).

Fithian, Philip Vickers (1747–1766). *Journal and Letters of Philip Vickers Fithian: A Plantation Tutor of the Old Dominion, 1773–1774*, ed. Hunder Dickinson Farish (Charlottesville: University of Virginia, 1957), and other editions. The 1900 edition is available online.

Franklin, Benjamin (1706–1790). *The Autobiography of Benjamin Franklin,* multiple editions. Available online.

Freeman, Hannah, also known as "Indian Hannah" (1731?–1802). Marshall Joseph Becker, "Legends About Hannah Freeman ("Indian Hannah"): Squaring the Written Accounts with the Oral Traditions," *Keystone Folklore* 4:2 (1992): 1–23. See also Marshall Joseph Becker, "Hannah Freeman: An Eighteenth-Century Lenape Living and Working Among Colonial Farmers," *PMHB* 114:2 (1990): 249–69.

Herbergs, Johannes (1717–1789). *Brave New World: Rhinelanders Conquer America,* ed. Dieter Pesch (Kommern: Martine Galunder-Verlag, 2001).

Harrower, John (1734–1776). *The Journal of John Harrower, an Indentured Servant in the Colony of Virginia,* ed. Edward Miles Riley (Williamsburg: Colonial Williamsburg, 1963).

Mittelberger, Gottlieb (1711–after 1754). *Journey to Pennsylvania,* ed. Oscar Handlin and John Clive (Cambridge, Mass.: Harvard University Press, 1960).

Katherine M. Faull, ed. and trans., *Moravian Women's Memoirs: Their Related Lives, 1750–1820* (Syracuse: Syracuse University Press, 1997).

Potter, Israel R. (1744-ca. 1824). *The Life and Remarkable Adventures of Israel R. Potter,* ed. Leonard Kriegel (1824; reprint, New York: Corinth Books, 1962).

Thewonya's [English: Chain or Awl Breaker], also known as Governor Blacksnake, (1753–1859). Thomas S. Abler, ed., *Chainbreaker: The Revolutionary War Memoirs of Governor Blacksnake as Told to Benjamin Williams* (Lincoln: University of Nebraska Press, 1989).

Whitehead, John Frederick, also known as Johann Friederick Kukuck, or Cuckoo (1757–1815), and Buettner, Johann Carl, also Buttner der Amerikaner (1754–182?). *Souls for Sale: The Autobiographies of Two German Redemptioners,* ed. Susan E. Klepp, Farley Grubb, and Anne Pfaelzer de Ortiz (University Park: The Pennsylvania State University Press, forthcoming).

Woolman, John (1720–1772). *The Journal of John Woolman and a Plea for the Poor,* ed. Frederick B. Tolles (Secaucus, N.J.: Citadel Press, 1961), and other editions.

Woomba, Ofodobendo, also known as York or Andrew the Moor (1729?–1779). Daniel B. Thorp, trans. and ed., "Chattel with a Soul: The Autobiography of a Moravian Slave," *PMHB* 112:3 (1988): 433–51.

THE
INFORTUNATE:

OR, THE

VOYAGE and ADVENTURES

OF

WILLIAM MORALEY,

Of MORALEY, in the County of *Northumberland*, Gent.

From his BIRTH, to the PRESENT TIME.

CONTAINING,

Whatever is curious and remarkable in the **Provinces of** *Penfilvania* and *New Jersey*; an Account of the **Laws and** Cuſtoms of the Inhabitants; the Product, Soil and Climate; alſo the AUTHOR's ſeveral Adventures through divers **Parts** of *America*, and his ſurpriſing Return to *Newcaſtle*.

To which is added,

His CASE, recommended to the Gentlemen of the Law.

Written by HIMSELF.

Felix quem faciunt aliena pericula cautum. HOR.
——— *Si quid noviſti rectius iſtis,*
Candidus imperti; ſi non, his utere mecum. HOR.

NEWCASTLE:

Printed by J. WHITE, for the AUTHOR; and ſold by the Bookſellers in Town and Country.

MDCCXLIII.

[EDITORS' NOTE: The title page of *The Infortunate*, reproduced on the other side of this page, was photographed by the William L. Clements Library, University of Michigan, and is used by permission. The word "infortunate" (rather than "unfortunate") was more commonly used in Shakespeare's time than later, during the eighteenth century. Moraley reserves "infortunate" for the title and uses the modern spelling in the body of his memoirs. It is possible that Moraley's choice of the word is based on the play *The Banish'd Duke; or, The Tragedy of Infortunatus* (London: Baldwin, 1690), a thinly disguised, anonymous account of the Duke of Monmouth's ill-fated attempt to overthrow James II in 1685. Like Moraley, Infortunatus is banished by his family. He bewails his fate in exile: "Whilst all my Forces (plainly to confess) / Are raw, unarm'd, and I am moneyless. / From sorrow's Scene I do contemplate now / What base deceitful peoples brought me to." And Moraley would have agreed with Infortunatus's politics and fatalism: "Since time began, ne're was a juster cause; / Than Lives, Religion, Liberty and Laws; / We fight for Heaven, our Kingdom, Church and State, / Submitting all we have to Divine Fate." (Quotations from pp. 20 and 28.)

The first epigraph on the title page, attributed to Horace, means "Happy is he who is warned by another's danger." It does not, however, come from Horace (see Dominicus Bo., *Lexicon Horatianum*, 2 vols. [Hildensheim: Georg Olms, 1965]). Benjamin Franklin used it as the heading for the following comic piece in *Poor Richard's Almanack for 1734*:

> *Felix quem faciunt aliena pericula cautum.*
> To such a height th' Expence of COURTS is gone,
> That poor Men are redress'd—*till they're undone.*

William, your Cause is good, give me my Fee, and I'll defend it. But, alas! William is cast, the Verdict goes against him. *Give me another Fee, and I'll move the Court in Arrest of Judgment.* Then Sentence is confirmed. *T'other Fee, and I'll bring a Writ of Error.* But judgment is again confirm'd, and *Will* condemn'd to pay Costs. What shall we do now, Master, says William. *Why since it can't be helpt, there's no more to be said; pay the Knave his Money, and I'm satisfied.*

> Of disposition they're most sweet,
> Their clients always kindly greet;
> And tho' at Bar they rip old Sores,
> And brawl and scold like drunken Wh——s,
> Their Angers in a moment pass
> Away at Night over a Glass;
> Nay often laugh at the Occasion
> Of their premeditated Passion.
> *O may you prosper as you treat us,*
> *Until the D——l sign your* Quietus.

Franklin borrowed his foreign language aphorisms from James Howell's *Lexicon Tetraglotton* of 1660. See Van Wyck Brooks, ed., *Poor Richard: The Almanacks for the Years 1733–1758* (New York: Ballantine, 1976), 23–24, 295.

The second epigraph is indeed from Horace (*Epistles*, 1.6.68: "To Numicus"). A contemporary translation of both lines is: "[Live and be happy.] If you know any maxims better than these, impart them with your usual candor; if not, make the best use you can of mine" (David Watson, *The Works of Horace Translated into English Prose*, 2 vols. [1739; reprint, New York: AMS, 1976], 2:232). This epigraph was commonly employed in eighteenth-century literature. Pope, Addison, Steele, Fielding, and Chesterfield used these lines in publications that appeared during Moraley's lifetime. See Caroline Grad, *Horace in the English Literature of the Eighteenth Century* (New Haven: Yale University Press, 1916).]

THE PREFACE

MY Design in prefixing this *Preface*, is to return the Worthy Gentlemen of *Newcastle*,[1] and Parts adjacent, my most sincere and hearty Thanks for the many Favours they have bestow'd on me, undeservedly. At present, I have no other Way to retaliate them; therefore hope they will accept of these my weak Endeavours, as a Specimen of my Gratitude.

There are in the following Pages many Observations to be found, which are not to be met with, perhaps, in other Authors; I having an Opportunity, the Time I was abroad, of conversing with the most substantial Planters, from whom I was inform'd of many Particulars relating to the Laws and Customs of the Provinces I resided in.

On the Whole, I have advanc'd nothing but what I know to be Truth, in however rough and homely a Dress it may happen to appear;

---

1. See Appendix E for more information about Newcastle.

and compos'd it, not only to reflect on the unhappy State of Life I was reduced to by my Inconsideration, but to persuade Mankind, that the only Way to avoid the like Difficulties, is to take care how they misapply their Talents, and endeavour to improve 'em to a better Purpose than the most unfortunate of Mankind.

W. MORALEY.

1 MORALEY AND HIS FAMILY—THE
INFORTUNATE LEARNS LATIN AND
ARITHMETIC—BOUND TO AN ATTORNEY—BECOMES
A WATCHMAKER—THE SOUTH SEA
BUBBLE—HIS MOTHER SETTLES IN
NEWCASTLE—REDUCED TO POVERTY—SELLS
HIMSELF FOR A TERM OF YEARS INTO THE
AMERICAN PLANTATIONS—BEFORE THE LORD MAYOR
OF LONDON—REPENTING TOO LATE—CALLING
AT CALAIS—A RECOGNITION.

THE Calamities that afflict human Nature are generally owing to the imprudent Management of their Affairs. A sad Instance of the Truth of this Reflection, the following Relation contains, which is communicated to the World, in order to induce Mankind to act with Caution and Discretion, that they may avoid the Inconveniences and Disappointments which attend the Unwary and Inconsiderate.

London is the Place of my Nativity, which was in the Year 1698. My Parents were of no mean Account, and in good Circumstances, my Father being the third and youngest Son of a Gentleman, Chief of an ancient Family and considerable Estate, descended from the Barons *Morley*, of *Swanton Morley*, in *Norfolk*. By Charter from King *Edward* I.[1] he held Lands in *Northumberland*, bearing his Name, which were increased by Purchase; and in the last Century were augmented by two Marriages, first by *William Moraley*, my Great Great Grandfather, with *Elizabeth*,

1. Edward I reigned from 1272 to 1307.

Daughter to *Nicolas Ridley*, of *Willemoteswick*, in *Com. Northumb'*, Esq;
and secondly, by *Agnes*, Daughter of *Alexander Ridley*, of *Whitsheals*,
third Brother of the said *Nicolas Ridley*, to *Thomas Moraley*, Son of the
above *William Moraley*.

By this Alliance, large Possessions were added to the Paternal Estate;
which passing from the Family by the Extravagance of my Father's elder
Brother, he was oblig'd to seek his Fortune, and became a Citizen of
London, where he married *Martha*, the Daughter of Mr *John Mason*, a
wealthy Founder and Citizen.[2] Her Mother, nam'd *Martha*, was Daughter of *Henry Stevens*, of *Steventon*, in *Com. Berks*,[3] Esq; allied to the Family
of *Sonds*, of *Lees Court*, in *Com. Cantii*,[4] in the Person of Sir *George Sonds*,
Knight of the Bath, afterwards created Earl of *Faversham* by King
Charles II.[5] whose eldest Daughter was married to *Lewis*, Marquis of
Blanquefort, Baron *Duras* in *England*, who, by the Death of Sir *George*,
became, by Reversion, Earl of *Faversham*, in right of his Wife. He was
second Brother to *Charles d'Urfort de Duras*, Duke and Marshal of *France*.
The second Daughter of Sir *George* married Sir *Lewis Watson*, afterwards
Lord *Rockingham*, Grandfather to the present Earl of *Rockingham*.

I mention this not out of Ostentation, but because some People have
represented her as meanly descended: For my part, I do not think true
Honour consists in an Alliance to a Coronet; but, on the contrary, they

---

2. Moraley's father served three masters in quick succession, finally spending seven years with
Thomas Tompion as an apprentice. Moraley achieved his freedom in 1688 and afterward was hired by
Tompion as a journeyman worker. The Office of the Archbishop of Canterbury in Knightrider Street,
London, issued the marriage license for Moraley's parents on November 24, 1697. The apprenticeship
of Moraley's father appears in Charles Edward Atkins, *Register of Apprentices of the Worshipful Company of
Clockmakers of the City of London from Its Incorporation in 1631 to Its Tercentenary in 1931* (Privately
printed, 1931), 203. Moraley's father gave a brief summary of his career when advertising his move from
London to Newcastle upon Tyne: "William Moraley, Clock and Watch-Maker, who served his
Time with, and wrought for the famous Mr. Tompion at London, till his Decease [November 20,
1713], is lately come into his Native Country, and designs to reside in Newcastle upon Tine, who
makes and sells Gold and Silver-Watches, mends and cleans all Sorts of Clocks or Watches; and is to be
met with at John Morley's House, next Door to the Black and the Grey, in the Big-Market, Newcastle"
(*Newcastle Weekly Courant*, August 24, 1723, 10–11). The date of the marriage license of Moraley's
parents is in George E. Cokayne and Edward Alexander Fry, eds., *The Index Library: Calendar of
Marriage Licenses Issued by the Faculty Office, 1632–1714* (London: By subscription, 1905), 153. William
Moraley's birth is recorded in Willoughby A. Littledale, ed., *The Registers of Christ Church, Newgate,
1538 to 1754*, Publications of the Harleian Society—Registers (London: Harleian Society, 1895), 21,
91.

3. Berkshire.

4. Kent.

5. Charles II reigned from 1680 to 1685.

Figure 1. *"Industry and Idleness*, 1: 'The Fellow 'Prentices at their Looms'" (William Hogarth, 1747). The two apprentices start their careers in identical circumstances, but one is industrious and the other is idle.

that behave themselves in the most virtuous and humble Manner, deserve the greatest Esteem.

In my Infancy, such care was taken of me, by an Education suitable to their Circumstances, as laid the Foundation of all the Evils that have since befallen me, by the over Indulgence of my Parents. In a more advanced Age, I was taught the *Latin* Tongue, with Arithmetick, besides Musick and Dancing. I had likewise an Opportunity of conversing with the *Royal Society*,[6] and by that Means have gone through several Courses of *Natural Philosophy*, by which I might have preferr'd myself; but being of too lively a Disposition, I neglected to improve my Talents, always preferring the present Time to the future; so that all these Advantages were bestow'd on me to no Purpose.

6. The Royal Society of London for Improving Natural Knowledge, founded in 1645.

Figure 2. *"Industry and Idleness*, 6: 'The Industrious 'Prentice out of his Time, & Married to his Master's Daughter'" (William Hogarth, 1747). The industrious apprentice advances in his profession by marrying the master's daughter.

    At 15 Years of Age, my Father bound me Clerk to an eminent Attorney in the Lord Mayor's Court,[7] where I continued near two Years; but my Father not liking the Profession of the Law, by reason of the many Quirks[8] and Shifts[9] used by the Gentlemen Practitioners, with the Advice of *Henry May*, Esq; Recorder of the City of *Chichester*, formerly a

7. Exercising both judicial and administrative functions, the Lord Mayor's Court was one of the most important in the country. It consisted of the mayor, aldermen, and a recorder and met in the King's Bench, Guildhall. See Walter Besant, *London in the Eighteenth Century* (London: Black, 1903), 201.

8. Subtleties, artful distinctions. E. L. McAdam Jr. and George Milne, eds., *Johnson's Dictionary: A Modern Selection* (New York: Pantheon, 1963), 327. All definitions are from this source unless otherwise noted.

9. Expedients found or used with difficulty.

Figure 3. *"Industry and Idleness*, 10: 'The Industrious 'Prentice, Alderman of London, the Idle one brought before him & Impeach'd by his Accomplice'" (William Hogarth, 1747). The two apprentices meet again when the idle one is apprehended for murder and brought to judgment before the industrious one, now Alderman of London.

Background

Spanish Merchant, join'd to that of *William Carr*, Esq;[10] a Commissioner of the Excise, and Member of Parliament for *Newcastle*, took me from my Employ, and learnt me the Trade of Watch-making.

In my Clerkship, I did little else but vapour[11] about the Streets, with my Sword by my Side; as for studying the Law, little of that serv'd me, my Time being taken up with pursuing the Pleasures of the Town: Company was the Thing I chiefly thought on, and how to support it; which my Father perceiving, being an austere Man, closely observ'd my

10. William Carr (d. 1742) was elected to Parliament from Newcastle as a Whig for the years 1722–27 and 1729–34. He also served as mayor of the city in 1724 and 1737. See Romney Sedgwick, *The House of Commons, 1715–1754*, 2 vols. (New York: Oxford, 1970), 1:532.

11. To bully or brag.

another sign of gentility

Figure 4. "An Emblematical Print on the South Sea Scheme" (William Hogarth, 1721). This engraving is an allegory of the rampant speculation in the South Sea Company, which failed in 1720. The work depicts investors consumed by a speculative frenzy at the expense of middle-class values of industry and frugality. A merry-go-round operated by the South Sea Company stands in the center. The guild hall (where Moraley's apprenticeship was changed from attorney to watchmaker) stands on the left. Having taken possession of Fortune, a devil butchers her and throws her flesh to the crowd.

Actions, and mildly told me the Inconveniencies that would arise, if I did not take up in time, and reform, such as Loss of Friends, and a general Contempt from Mankind. He calmly told me, if I would follow his Directions, he would give me all the Encouragement that lay in his Power, by advancing my Fortune when a proper Time offer'd; and added, that *Virtue carries along with it its own Reward.*[12] My coming home had this good Effect, that it took me from my former loose Companions, the Bane of Youth; and after this, I became tractable, and obedient to my Father's Commands.

12. William Moraley, the author, was apprenticed to his father on May 5, 1718, for an unspecified number of years; apparently he never completed his apprenticeship. See Atkins, *Register of Apprentices,* 204.

Figure 5.   Interior of a clockmaker's shop (Thomas Rowlandson, 1783). This provincial
English store contains large display windows, a glass case full of assembled watches, and a
comfortable chair for customers.

About this time, the World run mad after the *South Sea* Bubble.[13] My Father was bit to the Tune of £800, which somewhat impair'd his Fortune; and being advanc'd in Years, proposed to my Mother to settle at *Newcastle*, where he had many Friends. She declin'd this Proposal for some Years, but at last agreed to it, by my giving her a good Account of the Place, where I had been some Years before.

We arriv'd at *Newcastle* after two Days Sail, and settled for about two Years, meeting with Encouragement in our Business from the generous Inhabitants. In the meantime, my Father having Notice of the Death of his Brother, left us, in order to secure his Effects, but unfortunately died at *Harwich*, in his Passage home from *London*, in the Year 1725, from which Time I date all my Misfortunes. He had made a Will, which not answering my Expectations, occasioned frequent Quarrels and Contests between my Mother and myself; and her marrying again,[14] widen'd the Breach, and oblig'd me to leave *Newcastle* for *London*, where I arrived with 12 s[hillings] only, given me by my Mother, to *seek my Fortune*, she assuring me she could not raise any more, by reason of her Marriage.[15]

The Money being soon spent, and not readily falling into Business, I was reduc'd to Poverty. A Gentleman[16] let her know my Circumstances. She answer'd, she had given all out of her Power, and could do no more for me. He writ to her again, threatening her, if she did not restore the

13. Many Englishmen speculated wildly in the South Sea Company during the second decade of the eighteenth century. Although the company enjoyed a monopoly of trade in the South Seas, it was primarily a financial enterprise designed to assume the national debt and to use its credit to finance capital expansion. But the South Sea Company's directors, seeking to get rich quick, employed various shady means to inflate stock prices and realize large capital gains. The crash of 1720 ended the speculative frenzy, depleted the fortunes of many investors, and shook the government to its foundations. (Figure 4 is William Hogarth's engraving depicting the catastrophe of the South Sea Bubble.) See John Carswell, *The South Sea Bubble* (Stanford, Calif.: Stanford University Press, 1960); and J. H. Plumb, *The First Four Georges: England and Her "German" Kings, 1714–1830* (Boston: Little, Brown & Co., 1956), 62–64.

14. Martha Moralee married Charles Isaacson on October 19, 1728, at St. Andrew's Church in Newcastle. Isaacson, the son of Anthony and Jane Isaacson, was fifty-three years old, having been baptized in 1675 both at St. Nicholas Church in Newcastle and at a nonconformist church. (IGI.)

15. Married women did not exercise control over their property after their wedding unless a prenuptial agreement placed it in trust. Blackstone later summarized British law on the relations between husband and wife: "By marriage, the husband and wife are one person in law: that is, the very being or legal existence of the woman is suspended during the marriage. . . . [She] is therefore called in our law-French, a feme covert, and is said to be under the protection and influence of her husband, her baron, or lord; and her condition during her marriage is called her coverture" (J. W. Ehrlich, *Ehrlich's Blackstone, Part One: Rights of Persons, Rights of Things* [New York: Capricorn, 1959], 83).

16. Moraley's lawyer.

Figure 6.   The Second Royal Exchange. Moraley went here to find information about a passage to America.

third Part of the Personal Effects to me, he would do me Justice; and withal let her know, he had applied to the Chamber of *London* on my Account. She answer'd him, if he or I gave her Trouble, she would leave all she had a Right to, from me: So the Affair dropp'd. I had now my Ingenuity to trust to; and it was in vain to expect any Subsistence from her.

precedes a failure to 'pull himself up by his bootstraps' ale B. F.

The said Gentleman writ another Letter to her, and told her, it was needless to contend with me, for I was resolv'd to have my Right, notwithstanding my Father's Will, and any Release I could give her, unless she could prove I receiv'd my whole Fortune from her, a Release only standing good for so much as I had receiv'd, which was but £20 for the Acquittance of about £300 (for the Lord Mayor's Court being a Court of Equity, Remedy would be had against such an Imposition) and advised her to restore me the remainder.

But not hearing from her, I being resolute, as not caring what be-

came of me, it enter'd into my Head to leave *England*, and sell myself
for a Term of Years into the *American* Plantations. Accordingly I repair'd to the *Royal Exchange*, to inform myself, by the printed Advertisements fix'd against the Walls, of the Ships bound to *America*; where
musing by myself, a Man[17] accosted me in the following Manner. Sir,
said he, I have for some time observ'd you, and fancy your Condition of
Life is alter'd for the worse, and guess you have been in better Circumstances; but if you will take my Advice, I'll make it my Business to find
out some way which may be of Service to you. Perhaps you may imagine
I have a Design to inveigle you, but I assure you I have none; and if you
will accept of a Mug of Beer, I will impart what I have to propose to
you. The Man appearing sincere, I gave Ear to him.

I was dress'd at that Time in a very odd Manner. I had on a Red Rug[18]
Coat, with Black Lining, Black Buttons and Button Holes, and Black
Lace upon the Pockets and Facing; an old worn out Tye Wig, which
had not been comb'd out for above a Fortnight; an unshaven Beard; a
torn Shirt, that had not been wash'd for above a Month; bad Shoes; and
Stockings all full of Holes.

After he had shav'd me, he proposed to me an *American* Voyage, and
said there was a Ship at *Limehouse* Dock, that would sail for *Pensilvania*
in three or four Days. Sir, said I, a Person like me, oppress'd by Dame
Fortune, need not care where he goes. All Places are alike to me; and I
am very willing to accept of your Offer, if I could have some View of
bettering my Condition of Life, though I might have expected a better
Fate than to be forc'd to leave my Native Country: But adverse Fortune

---

17. According to the servitude contract for "William Morley" recorded on October 13, 1729, the
man was Neal MacNeal. Moraley's destination is given as the Caribbean island of Antigua, but this
merely indicates that MacNeal sent the bulk of his recruits to that destination. Historian John Wareing
explains: "After 1724 it appears to have been the practice of the clerks who made up the register to take
a bundle of indenture forms drawn up by an agent during a particular month and to enter the destination from just one of them as the destination for the whole group, even when a variety of destinations
were involved." MacNeal did file Moraley's indenture along with a number of others. Moraley's name
was spelled "Morley" on the contract, but, as Wareing and numerous other historians have noted, there
was no standard spelling of surnames in the eighteenth century. The family itself used or tolerated
variant spellings, including Moraley, Moreley, Morley, Morrowley, Moralee, and Morralee. The name
is spelled both as Moraley and as Morley in the two surviving signatures of Moraley's mother. His
father's will contains three different variants of the surname. Still, it is possible that the extant indenture contract is not the one signed by the author of these memoirs. See John Wareing, *Emigrants to
America: Indentured Servants Recruited in London, 1718–1733* (Baltimore: Genealogical Publishing Co.,
1985); quotations on 8–9, 77.

18. A coarse woolen cloth.

GREAT BRITAIN AND IRELAND

SCOTLAND

NEWCASTLE

IRELAND

ENGLAND

HARWICH

LONDON

FRANCE

**Moraley's Outward
Bound Journey**

1. Erith
2. Gravesend
3. Nore Light House
4. Deal and Goodwin Sands
5. Calais
6. Dover
7. Plymouth
8. Eddystone Light House
9. Lizard Point

**Moraley's Homeward
Bound Journey**

10. Cape Clear
11. Cork
12. Kinsale
13. Dublin
14. Whitehaven
15. Carlingford
16. Isle of Man
17. Workington

Map 1. Great Britain and Ireland.

is become familiar to me, by a Series of Misfortunes; so had rather leave
a Place where I have no Prospect of advancing myself, than to continue
here where I have no Friends to relieve me. Besides, in a distant Place,
not being known, no Person can reflect on me for any ill Management,
which oftentimes discourages one's Friends from supporting one, knowing the ill Use that is made of their Support.

Sir, says the Person, I'm entirely of your Way of Thinking, and
believe you will better yourself by following my Advice. I will recom-
mend you to the Captain, who is bound for *Philadelphia*, in *Pennsilvania*, a Country producing everything necessary for the Support of Life;
and when your Time is expir'd, you will be free to live in any of the
Provinces of *America*.

Then he ask'd me, if I was bred to any Business. I told him, Watch-
making was my Occupation. He said, he was afraid I would not do for
any other Business, that being of little Service to the *Americans*; the
useful Trades being, Bricklayers, Shoemakers, Barbers, Carpenters,
Joiners, Smiths, Weavers, Bakers, Tanners, and Husbandmen more useful than all the rest.[19] They bind themselves for four Years; but if I
would consent to bind myself for five, he said he would undertake to
get me admitted. Those Men Brokers have generally for their Pains
Three Half Crowns,[20] given them by the Masters of those Vessels which
they are employ'd for.

After we had drank two Pints of Beer, he paid the Reckning. I abso-
lutely agreed to go, and to that Intent we went before Sir *Robert Bailis*,[21]
Lord Mayor, where I was sworn as not being a married Person, or an
Apprentice by Indenture. He paid for my Oath one Shilling, a Per-
quisite[22] of his Clerk. From thence we went to *London-Bridge*, to a Sta-
tioner's Shop, and there an Indenture of Servitude was drawn, which I

19. Workers skilled in construction and agriculture and in making shoes and clothing were in great
demand in most parts of America; see David W. Galenson, "Labor Market Behavior in Colonial America: Servitude, Slavery, and Free Labor," in David W. Galenson, ed., *Markets in History: Economic Studies
of the Past* (Cambridge: Cambridge University Press, 1989), 65–66. Daniel Kent, an indentured servant
who emigrated to Pennsylvania a half-century after Moraley, believed that similar occupations remained
in demand in the region (Ella K. Barnard, comp., *Letters and Other Papers of Daniel Kent, Emigrant and
Redemptioner* [Baltimore, 1904], 17).

20. A half crown equaled 2 shillings and 6 pence.

21. Robert Baylis was mayor from 1728 to 1729. See Alfred B. Beaven, *The Aldermen of the City of
London, Temp. Henry III.—1912*, 2 vols. (London: Fisher, 1913), 2:124.

22. Something gained by a place or office in addition to wages.

sign'd.[23] After this we took [a] Boat at *Billingsgate*, steer'd our Course for *Limehouse*, where we arriv'd about Eleven o'Clock in the Forenoon. The Ship was named the *Bonetta*, of about 200 Tons; the Owner *Charles Hankin*, [and] *James Reed*, Commander. There were on board 20 Persons, all Men, bound to the same Place, and on the same Account. As soon as I enter'd, my Friend left me to think better on it, and wish'd me a prosperous Voyage, and a good Wife. ?

I observ'd several of my Brother Adventurers seem'd very dejected, from whence I guess'd they repented of their Rashness. Soon after, Dinner was brought on the Table, which consisted of stew'd Mutton Chops. I was very glad I had an Opportunity of trying the Temper of my Tusks, for I had not eaten any Meat for four Days. I eat very heartily, and wash'd down the mutton with about two Quarts of Small Beer.[24] I began to think myself happy, in being in a Way to eat; and on this Account, became insensible of the Condition I had brought myself to. In the Afternoon, the Master and Mate being absent, I ventur'd into the Cabin, and peeping into a Chest, discover'd a large Quantity of Raisins, of which I made free with about two Pound, and pocketed them for my own Use: Besides, the Small Beer stood upon Deck, and was free for us at all times; so that laying all Reflections [aside], I comforted myself with the Hopes of living well all the Voyage, but was soon made sensible to the contrary when we set out to Sea.

---

23. The standard printed form for an indenture was as follows:

> London ff. These are to certify, that (name, residence, age, occupation) came before me one of His Majesty's Justices of Peace, and Voluntarily made Oath that (he/she) this Deponent (is) not Married, nor Apprentice nor Covenant, or Contracted Servant to any Persons, nor listed Soldier or Sailor in His Majesty's Service, and (is) free and willing to serve (agent's name) or his Assigns (#) Years in (place) His Majesty's Plantation in *America*, and that (he/she is) not perswaded, or enticed so to do, but that it is (his/her) own Voluntary Act.
>
> (signature of servant)
>
> Jurat (date)
> Coram me (signature of the justice of the peace)

Aside from stipulating the length of service, the standard contract provided no protections for the servant. Assurances of "necessary Cloaths, Meat, Drink, Washing and Lodging" appeared only in the contracts of minors. Additional guarantees for adult servants rarely were included. David Galenson, *White Servitude in Colonial America: An Economic Analysis* (Cambridge: Cambridge University Press, 1981), 200–203.

24. Beer with little alcoholic content.

funny to
include
this in
memoir

The next Day I writ a Letter to one Mr *Stafford*, in *Old Fish-street*,[25] to let him know where I was, and whither bound. I sent it by the Mate's Wife, who deliver'd it to him. After he read the Letter, he bid her tell me, that I deserv'd all possible Hardships for my Imprudence, in leaving him at a time when he was doing me Justice, by prosecuting my Mother.

Three Days after, being under Sail, a Boat hail'd us, and the Boatman ask'd if there was not one *Moraley* on board. The Mate denied I was there; but was answer'd, there was an Order from the Lord Mayor to bring him back again. To which he replied, I was gone, the Captain having discharg'd me. So the Boatman was satisfied, and return'd. I was then fast asleep below, and the rest of the People were kept under Deck, to prevent their Knowlege of this Enquiry; which when I was made acquainted with, I curs'd my Fate ten thousand times.

That Evening we sail'd down the River for the *Nore*, and arriv'd at *Eriff*, where we took in fresh Provisions, and the next Morning anchor'd close to *Gravesend*. A Custom House Officer came on board, and demanded of us, one by one, whether we were forced against our Wills, or if we went voluntarily. There every Adventurer had his Apparel given him for the Voyage, which was, a Sea Jacket, two coarse chequ'd Shirts, a Woollen Waistcoat, two coarse Handkerchiefs, one Pair of Hose, a Woollen Cap, and a pair of bad new Shoes. Thus accoutr'd, we set Sail for *America*, with a fair Wind, on the 7th day of *September*, in the Year 1729.

The next Day we arriv'd at the *Downs*, and discover'd *Goodwin* Sand, and cast Anchor before *Deal* Castle.[26] The same Day the Captain mann'd a Boat for *Calais*, to buy Brandy. I begg'd of him to be one, for Curiosity's Sake; and after some Difficulty he granted me my Request. We arriv'd there after three Hours Sail, and on our Landing were civilly receiv'd by the Garrison. We bought a considerable Quantity of Brandy, they giving us a large Bowl of Punch for laying out Money. The Garrison at that Time consisted of 5000 Men, meanly clad, and as poorly

25. Old Fish Street was an extension of Knightrider Street and is now called by the latter name. See Eilert Ekwall, *Street-Names of the City of London* (Oxford: Clarendon Press, 1954), 74.

26. Ships often stopped at the town of Deal to take on supplies and to drop off the pilot. See Peter Kalm, *The America of 1750: Peter Kalm's Travels in North America*, ed. Adolph B. Benson, 2 vols. (New York: Dover, 1964), 1:1; and Edward Miles Riley, ed., *The Journal of John Harrower: An Indentured Servant in the Colony of Virginia, 1773–1776* (Williamsburg, Va.: Colonial Williamsburg, 1963), 29. See also Map 1.

fed. *Calais* is pretty strong by Art, made so purely to prevent a sudden Surprise from the *English*.

After two Hours Stay we return'd to the Ship, and the next Day perceiv'd *Goodwin* Sands beat higher than usual, which afforded a dismal Sight. Those Sands were once firm Land, adjoining to *Kent*, but were destroy'd in the Reign of *Edward* the Confessor[27] (about 700 Years ago), being then in the Possession of *Goodwin* Earl of *Kent*, Father to *Harold* II, King of *England*, but routed by *William*, Duke of *Normandy*, at the Battle of *Hastings*. Here we saw Droves of Purpoises playing in the Waves.

We then sail'd towards *Dover*, where we anchor'd. The Castle is a noble Range of Building. A Boat was sent off to fetch some more Provisions; which returning, brought on board three Gentlemen to see our Captain. One of them was nam'd *Sonds*, a Relation of Sir *George Sonds*.[28] He knew me at first Sight, and at my Desire related to the Company the unfortunate Story of Sir *George's* two Sons, which is as follows.

27. Edward the Confessor reigned from 1042 to 1066. William the Conqueror, victorious at the Battle of Hastings in 1066, became the first Norman monarch (1066–87).

28. Sir George Sondes, Earl of Feversham, 1600–1677, was the son of Sir Richard (not Michael) Sondes, and he was married in 1632 to Jane Freeman, daughter and heiress of Sir Ralph Freeman, Lord Mayor of London in 1633–34. The murder took place, as Moraley relates, on August 7, 1655. The case became celebrated as pamphleteers debated whether the father was the real culprit for having, as some claimed, "mismanaged his sons' education." See Leslie Stephen and Sidney Lee, eds., *Dictionary of National Biography*, 22 vols. (London: Oxford, 1917), 18:669–70.

THIS Gentleman was the Son of Sir *Michael Sonds*, of *Lees Court*. He married the Daughter of Alderman *Freeman*, Lord Mayor of *London*; by her he had two Sons, the Elder named *George*, the Younger *Freeman*. His Estate was £7000 *per Ann.* in *Kent*, and at *Sonds-place*, in *Surrey*, he had £2500 *per Annum* more. His Sons had an Education suitable to their Birth, and after they had pass'd through their several Studies, remain'd with their Father, and for some time liv'd in the Bands of Amity; but an unlucky Accident disturb'd the Peace of the Family. The elder Brother fell in Love with a young Lady named *Anne Delaune*, Niece to Sir *George*, living with one Mr *Hugginson*, a Gentleman in the Neighbourhood, and a Relation. This Affair coming to the Father's Ears, he order'd his Son to leave off all Thoughts of such a Match, for that God would not bless it, on account of their Nearness of Blood. But he being under-hand solicited by the Lady's Friends, renew'd his Addresses; when Mr *Hugginson* acquainting his Father with it by Letter, he came to the House, and finding them together, laid his strict Commands on the Son

not to proceed in his Amour, on pain of his Displeasure; then address-
ing himself to the Lady, said, He would get her a Husband in a proper
Time. After this, Mr *George* not only left off all Conversation, but
seem'd even to have an Aversion for her; and ever after was obedient to
his Father.

About this Time young *Freeman* took a Fancy to a Lady, who was
reported to have several Hundreds *per Annum*, and he proposed it to his
Father; but he evading the Matter, made the Son the more assiduous,
upon which his Father seemed to comply; but his Proposals not answering the Expectation of her Friends, the Match was broke of[f]: And
Sir *George* telling him, he must think no more of Marriage, for he design'd him for the Inns of Court, where he should be well provided for,
excited in him a disgust and hatred to his Brother, which caused frequent Quarrels between them; which the Father perceiving, told *Freeman*, that if he did not behave himself better to his Brother, he would
disinherit him, as his Father had served his Uncle *Nicolas*; and that it
was from his Brother he must expect his Fortune. This Discourse of the
Father had no Effect on him, but from that Instant he formed a Design
to kill his Brother that he might be the only Heir. One Night as they
lay together he got out of Bed, and went into an adjoining Room, and
took from thence a Cleaver and a Stilletto, a kind of Italian Poignard,
with the first he clove his Head, and stabbed him in the Breast with the
Stilletto; after which he went into his Father's Bed Chamber, and awak-
ing him, said, *Sir, I have kill'd my Brother*. The Gentleman heard a
Noise, but did not expect any such mischance, but arising, went with
him into the Room, where he saw his Son not quite dead, weltering in
his Blood. The next Morning the Affair got Wind. He was apprehended
by the Officers of Justice, and committed to *Maidstone* Jail, where he
remain'd along time till the Assizes, was then arraign'd for the Murder,
which he confess'd, and became remarkable for his Repentance; but notwithstanding his Father's Interest, who got him repriev'd from time to
time, he was hanged for the same; whereby an ancient noble Family, for
want of direct Male Heirs, is extinct.

T HE Gentlemen being gone ashore, we soon after set sail for *Plymouth*; in two Days got into the Harbour, and anchor'd in *Cat Water*, where we moored our Ship. *Plymouth* is a strong Town, with a Fort, and Garrison, with four Companies of Soldiers. There one of our Adventurers made his escape, by swimming to Shore. We took in fresh Provision at this Place for the last time, a favourable Wind arising, we took the Advantage, and passed by *Eddistone* Lighthouse, steering our course toward the *Lizard* Point, which altered our Way of living for the Worse, for we were stinted in our Allowance, being joined together in Messes: Five to each Mess. Three Biscuits were given to each Man for the Day, and a small Piece of Salt Beef, no bigger then a Penny Chop of Mutton. Some Days we had Stockfish,[1] when every Man was obliged to

---

1. Dried cod, so called from its hardness.

beat his Share with a Maul to make it tender, with a little stinking Butter for Sauce.[2]

Every Morning and Evening the Captain called every one of us to the Cabbin Door, where we received a Thimble full of bad Brandy. We were obliged to turn out every four Hours, with the Sailors, to watch; which was to prevent our falling sick, by herding under Deck.

In our Voyage we observed little worth taking Notice of, till we were in Latitude 33,[3] when the Sun was intensely hot, which so partch'd our Bodies, having but a scanty Allowance of Water, not above three Quarts to each Mess. We attempted to drink the Salt Water, but it increased our Thirst. Sometimes, but rarely, it rained, when we set our Hats upon Deck to catch the Water; but it sliding down the Sails, gave it the Taste of Tarr.

We catched several Dolphins and flying Fish. They caught them thus: With a Weapon called by them a *Fizgig*, like the Fangs of *Neptune's* Trident, fixed to a long Pole and at the other End tied by a Rope fast to the Ship's Stern. When the Fish arrives near the Surface of the Water, they strike the Instrument downright, and having hooked the Fish, give it time to weary itself in the Water, to prevent his breaking the Line. For Goodness it surpasses a Cod.

The Dolphins Food is Flying Fish, who are so much afraid of them, that they scarce dare venture to dip themselves in the Water for fear of being caught by them, they being often oblig'd to wet their Wings, otherwise they would be dry, which prevents their Flying. They seldom rise above two or three Foot above the Surface, tho' I have seen them, when their Wings fail them, drop upon the Deck. They are about the Largeness of a Pilchard, and are good Food. I have eaten of them.

I had forgot the Magnitude of the Dolphins, they are generally one Foot and a Quarter long, flatter than a Salmon, and in the Water for Beauty exceed all the Fishes in the Ocean, having diversity of Colours,

---

2. Indentured servants sometimes received meager rations during the ocean voyage. John Harrower noted that the bondsmen on his ship almost mutinied when the captain initially notified them of their food allowance, and that two servants were shackled in irons for complaining about their diets during the voyage (*Journal of John Harrower*, 20). Farley Grubb, however, concluded that ship captains likely provided good dietary fare in order to deliver healthy servants who would bring a high price ("Redemptioner Immigration to Pennsylvania: Evidence on Contract Choice and Profitability," *Journal of Economic History* 46 [1986]: 407–18).

3. Latitude 33 runs north of Charleston, South Carolina, and south of Casablanca, Morocco.

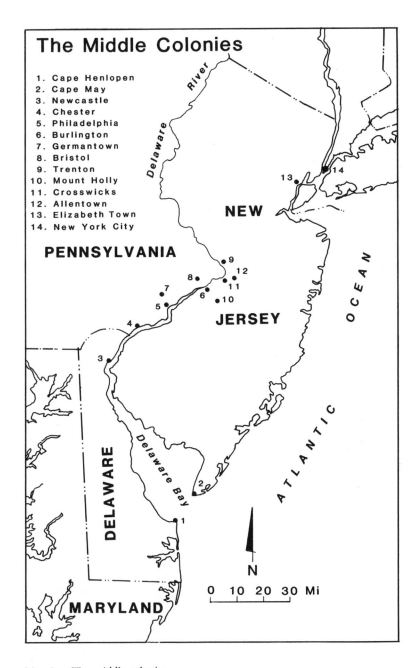

Map 2. The middle colonies.

of which Gold is the Principle, which by its shining, gives the flying Fish an Opportunity of avoiding them.

We saw several Land Birds at the Distance of fifteen hundred Miles from Land. When tired, they oftentimes alight on the Ship Masts, when they are easily taken. It is wonderful how they live so far from their proper Element, for when taken, being almost starved, they will eat unmercifully, but die soon after.

Every Day we discover'd a kind of Moss swimming upon the Sea, which plainly proved we were not far from the Gulph of *Mexico*, where it only grows.[4] We having hitherto used the Benefit of the *Monsoons*, or *Trade Winds*,[5] were obliged to steer for a more Northern Latitude, and very sensibly felt an Alteration in the Climate, which soon after became Cold. We got within Soundings, which we found by our Plummets, and discovered the *American* Coast, being *Cape Finlope*,[6] at the entrance of *Delaware* Bay, *Cape May* being opposite on the *New Jersey* Side.

We render'd God thanks for his Mercy in bringing us through so many Hardships, and prepair'd to sail up [the] *Delaware* River, so called from Capt. *Delaware*,[7] who first discovered it. In order to our more safe passing, there being many Rocks at the first Enterance, we took a Pilot; and in three Tides, after passing by *Newcastle* and *Chester*, arrived at *Philadelphia*, the day after *Christmas* Day.[8]

We drank so freely of the River Water, which, having a Purgative

4. The Sargasso Sea, characterized by the brown seaweed of its name, extends as far east as the Azores and is bounded on the west and north by the Gulf Stream.

5. The northeast trade winds would have carried the ship in a southwesterly direction toward the Caribbean, and the Westerlies would have carried it north along the North American coast.

6. Cape Henlopen, not Finlope, in Delaware (see Map 2).

7. Thomas West, third Lord de la Warr, landed briefly at the mouth of the river now bearing his name in 1611.

8. Moraley is mistaken about the date. The ship actually entered the port of Philadelphia during the week of December 9–16, 1729, according to reports in both the city's newspapers, the *Pennsylvania Gazette* (see Figure 7) and the *American Weekly Mercury*, for that week. Moraley thus spent thirteen weeks journeying from Gravesend to Philadelphia, about average for ocean passage at the time. After spending three weeks in Philadelphia, Moraley may have reached his new home in Burlington, New Jersey, on the day after Christmas, as he recalled. This chronology agrees with Moraley's subsequent comment that his first night in Burlington was the first time he had slept in a bed for fifteen weeks. Edward Horne and William Rawle, the two men who offered servants for sale from the ship on which Moraley arrived (see Figure 7), were Quaker merchants in the city (see Gary B. Nash, "The Early Merchants of Philadelphia," in Richard S. Dunn and Mary Maples Dunn, eds., *The World of William Penn* [Philadelphia: University of Pennsylvania Press, 1986], 360–61). The *Boneta* left Philadelphia for London during the first week of the new year, according to the *Pennsylvania Gazette* and the *American Weekly Mercury*, December 30–January 6, 1730, issues.

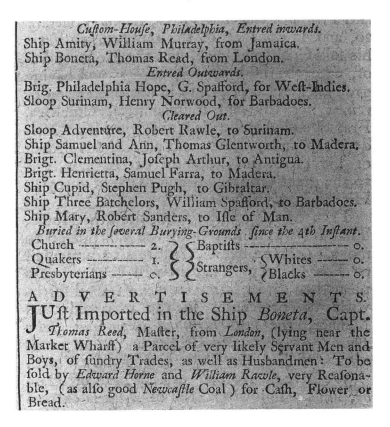

Figure 7. Newspaper notice of the arrival of the ship *Boneta* and advertisement of servants for sale, *Pennsylvania Gazette* (Philadelphia), December 9–16, 1729. Moraley arrived on this ship and was among the servants advertised to be sold.

Quality, caused some of us to fall Sick. I got a Diabates,[9] that brought me so low, that being reduced to a very weak Condition, I was forced to drink Rum, which drying up and strengthening the urinary Vessels, after three Months was cured.

We all of us had the Liberty of Visiting the Town, where I sold my

9. "Diabetes" is a term meaning the excessive production of urine. Samuel Johnson defined it as "a morbid copiousness of urine; a fatal colliquation by the urinary passages." It is now associated with either diabetes mellitus, caused by insufficient insulin production of the pancreas, or diabetes insipidus, a disorder of the pituitary gland. None of these descriptions fits Moraley's problem, which he claims to have cured through three months of drinking rum.

Red Coat for a Quart of Rum, my Tie Wig for Sixpence, with which I bought a Three-penny Loaf, and a Quart of Cyder.[10] Our Cargo consisting chiefly of Voluntary Slaves, who are the least to be pitied, I saw all my Companions sold of[f] before me; my turn came last, when I was sold for eleven Pounds, to one Mr *Isaac Pearson*,[11] a Man of Humanity, by Trade a Smith, Clock-maker and Goldsmith, living at *Burlington*, in *New Jersey*: He was a Quaker, but a Wet one.[12]

During my stay at *Philadelphia*, which was three Weeks, I had an Opportunity to survey one of the most delightful Cities upon Earth. As I was one Day amusing myself with the Prospect from the Water, being in a Poetick Strain, I hammered out the following Rhyme. The Reader must not expect from me a fine Performance, but such as it is, I freely give.[13]

10. That Moraley was allowed to leave the ship and wander about the city before he was sold was not typical. Just one year earlier a few servants absconded while roving around Philadelphia before they were auctioned, prompting most captains to confine servants to their ships until they had been purchased. See Farley Grubb, "The Auction of Redemptioner Servants, Philadelphia, 1771–1804: An Economic Analysis," *Journal of Economic History* 45 (1985): 585.

11. Isaac Pearson (ca. 1685–1749) was a blacksmith, silversmith, goldsmith, button manufacturer, ironmaster, and master watchmaker and clockmaker. Active in politics, he served as a state assemblyman, as state assay master for weights and measures, and as seal master. He married Hannah Gardiner in 1710, and they had three daughters, Rebecca, Elizabeth, and Sarah, who survived to adulthood. In 1746, he wed Rebecca Lovett, the widow of Samuel Scattergood, and she brought five minor children to the marriage. See Charles J. Burton, "A New Jersey Clock," *Bulletin of the National Association of Watch and Clock Collectors* 8 (1958): 213–14; Julia Sabine, "Silversmiths of New Jersey, 1623–1800," *Proceedings of the New Jersey Historical Society* 61 (1943): 252–55; Charles S. Boyer, *Early Forges and Furnaces in New Jersey* (Philadelphia: University of Pennsylvania Press, 1931), 128–29; William E. Drost, *Clocks and Watches of New Jersey* (Elizabeth, N.J.: Engineering Publishers, 1966), 192–201; and Carl M. Williams, *Silversmiths of New Jersey, 1700–1825, with Some Notice of Clockmakers Who Were Also Silversmiths* (Philadelphia: McManus, 1949), 34–45. See also "An Analysis of the Isaac Pearson Tall Clock in the Vauxhall Room, Winterthur," report from the Winterthur Museum Library, Delaware, May 1986; and Elaine Brenchley, "Isaac Pearson: Clockmaker of Burlington, West Jersey," Apprentice Guide Paper, Winterthur Museum Library, June 1982, both photocopied typescripts deposited at the Burlington County Historical Society. See Figure 14 for a clock produced in Pearson's shop.

12. A "wet" Quaker was a worldly member of the Society of Friends, a person whose behavior was not as austere, plain, and spiritual as those who adhered more strictly to the faith. Gaiety and attention to fashion characterized many wet Quakers. See Frederick B. Tolles, *Meeting House and Counting House: The Quaker Merchants of Colonial Philadelphia, 1682–1783* (Chapel Hill: University of North Carolina Press, 1948), 142–43.

13. Moraley cribbed most of this poem from one written by George Webb that appeared in Titan Leed, *The Genuine Leed's Almanac for . . . 1730* (Philadelphia: Leeds, 1730). However, Moraley shortened, rewrote, and added some original lines to the poem. On Webb, see David S. Shields, "The Wits and Poets of Pennsylvania: New Light on the Rise of Belles Lettres in Provincial Pennsylvania, 1720–1740," *PMHB* 109 (1985): 122–33. See also Appendix D for a full version of the original poem.

Key:

1. The Governours House
2. Quakers Meeting
3. The Market House
4. Where the Ships are built
5. Coopers Ferry
6. The Island
7. Society Hill
8. Wickacove
9. The Sweeds Church
10. Part of Gloster

Figure 8. "The Prospect of Philadelphia from Wickacove, exactly Delineated by G. Wood" (G. Wood, 1735). Although somewhat fanciful, this is the sole surviving depiction of the city at the time of Moraley's journey.

Goddess of Numbers, who art wont to rove
O'er the gay Landskip, and the smiling Grove:
Assist the soaring Muse, with Judgment to repeat.
The various Beauties of Thy Fav'rite Seat;
Thy Streets and Lanes, how regular and fair,
With thee no earthly City may compare.
While *Europe* groans, distress'd by hostile War,
No fears disturb the industrious Planters Care:
No unjust Sentence we have cause to fear;
No arbitrary Monarch rules us here.
Our Laws, our Liberties, and all are ours,
Our happy Constitution here secures,
The Seers, how cautious! and how gravely wise!
The hopeful Youth in Emulation rise;
Who, if the aspiring Muse does rightly sing,
Shall liberal Arts to such Perfection bring,
That *Europe* shall mourn, her antient Fame declin'd,
And *Philadelphia* shall be the *Athens* of Mankind.
What Praise, O Pen![14] what Thanks are due to thee!
For this first perfect Scheme of Liberty!
What Praise! what Thanks! to thee, O Pen! are given,
Beloved of Men! and Candidate for Heaven.

This famous City, is in the 40 Degree of Northern Latitude, and seated close to the Banks of [the] *Delaware*, which is here above one Mile broad,[15] and affords a fine Prospect on both Sides of it, there being great Numbers of fine Seats along its Banks, surrounded by pleasant Walks, and great Variety of different Sorts of Land, as Woods, Groves, verdant Fields, and Meadows. The Town stands on level Ground, which extends to seven or eight Miles in Circumference:[16] A charming Country it is, producing the most delectable Fruits of different Kinds, which

14. William Penn (1644–1718) was Proprietor of Pennsylvania from 1681 until his death.

15. The Delaware River at Market Street is still almost three-quarters of a mile broad, but the shores have been extended by developers since Moraley's day. Peter Kalm, a Swedish scientist, estimated the width of the Delaware River at Philadelphia as three-quarters of a mile in 1748 (Kalm, *America of 1750*, 1:27).

16. Moraley overestimates the city's circumference, which was probably much closer to three or four miles.

Figure 10.   Christ Church, Philadelphia.

grow in great Abundance, and are common to the weary Traveller, as well as the wealthy Citizen, it being no Trespass to gather them.

There are many Houses of Entertainment, at convenient distance from the Town, where the Inhabitants resort, in the cool Evenings, after the Fatigues of Business, where they regale themselves with the Product of this fertile Soil. This City is as large as *Bristol*, in *England*, but not so populous; and contains about 25,000 People,[17] who have Shops and Houses as handsome as those at *Newcastle upon Tyne*. The Streets are long and strait, and are called by these Names, *First Street, Second Street, Third Street, Fourth Street, Water Street*, lying along the Water, *Chestnut Street, Walnut Street, Front Street*, beside a good Number of Allies; as, *Mulberry Ally, Strawberry Ally, Black Horse Ally*, &c.

At the Upper-End of *Second Street*, is a State House,[18] for the Meeting of the Governor and Assembly, but not quite finished when I was there, which when done would be the finest Edifice in all *America*. The Market-place has a handsome House in it, where the Assembly sat, till the other was finished; this Fronts the River. In the Shambles[19] of this Market are sold all Kinds of Butchers Meat, as well cut and drest as at *London*: The Market Days are *Wednesdays* and *Saturdays*; but they have a Custom of retaling their Meat on *Sundays*, which is observed all over *America* in the Summer Time, because of the Heat of the Weather; Hens, Chickens, and Wild Fowl, are vended, with Poultry of all Kinds, and Fruits and Herbs.

The Houses are all of Brick, well sashed and glazed, and covered with white Cedar, more durable than Tiles.[20] The Oldest House in the Place, when I was there, being not above 49 Years standing. The Mayor has the Management of the Affairs, as chief Magestrate; but if he refuse to

17. The city and suburbs contained approximately 8,000 inhabitants in 1734. See Billy G. Smith, "Death and Life in a Colonial Immigrant City: A Demographic Analysis of Philadelphia," *Journal of Economic History* 37 (1977): 863–83; and P. M. G. Harris, "The Demographic Development of Colonial Philadelphia in Some Comparative Perspective," in Susan E. Klepp, ed., *The Demographic History of the Philadelphia Region, 1600–1860* (Philadelphia: American Philosophical Society, 1989), also published as a volume in *Proceedings of the American Philosophical Society* 133 (1989): 262–304.

18. Construction on the State House, now better known as Independence Hall, was begun in 1732, but the building was not occupied until 1741. See Edwin B. Bronner, "Village into Town, 1701–1746," in Russell F. Weigley, ed., *Philadelphia: A 300-Year History* (New York: W. W. Norton, 1982), 52–53.

19. Slaughterhouse.

20. Moraley exaggerates here, because many of the city's homes were constructed of stone or wood (Kalm, *America of 1750*, 1:19–20). Not until 1795 did a city ordinance require that buildings in the center of the city must be fabricated of brick.

Figure 11.   Stone Prison, southwest corner of Third and High Streets, Philadelphia.

do Justice, an Appeal lyes against him, to the Governor, who never fails to do Justice, he being a Man of an universal Character: He is a *Scotchman*, by Name *Gordon*,[21] and was a Major in Queen *Anne's* Army.[22]

The Religion professed here is of several Kinds: The *Establish'd* has the Preheminence, and has a large Church with an Organ. The *Quakers*, singly, are the most Numerous, who have two large Meetings; but if the *Presbyterians, Independents, Baptists, Papists* and *Freethinkers*, be joined to the Church Party, then the *Quakers* are not half the Number of the Inhabitants.[23]

21. Major Patrick Gordon served as the lieutenant governor of Pennsylvania from 1726 to 1736.

22. Queen Anne reigned from 1702 to 1714.

23. By "Establish'd" Moraley means the Church of England, although that church enjoyed no special legal status under Pennsylvania law. The Anglicans began construction of Christ Church (see Figure 10) in 1727 and completed it in 1744. The Quakers (Society of Friends) may have formed the largest religious group in the county, but burial statistics indicate that the number of Church of England members in the city was larger. The Presbyterians encompassed various English-speaking Calvinist groups, while the Baptists were a long-established but small congregation in the city. The "Papists," or Roman Catholics, had held services in Philadelphia since 1720, but they did not build a chapel until 1733. "Freethinkers" were not attached to any church and, based on burial statistics for 1730–32, accounted for as much as one-third of the population. Slaves comprised many of the residents not affiliated with any church. Moraley ignores the non-British religious groups, such as the Swedish Lutheran, German Lutheran, and German Reformed congregations active in the city at this time. See Bronner, "Village into Town," 47–53; and Susan E. Klepp, *"The Swift Progress of Population": A Documentary and Bibliographic Study of Philadelphia's Growth* (Philadelphia: American Philosophical Society, 1991), 46–47.

Here is a Lodge of the Society of Free and Accepted Masons. The principal Houses are Mr *Andrew Hamilton's*,[24] a *Scotch* Gentleman, who retired from *Scotland* for unfortunately killing his Brother[, and] *Israel Pemberton*,[25] a wealthy Quaker, of great Probity. The Post House is kept by Mr *Andrew Bradford*,[26] where he has a Printing House. At the End of the Town is *Society Hill*,[27] a pleasant Place, and a House of Entertainment, where I have spent many a Pound; it lies in the Road to *Scuylkill*.[28] I had forgot the Prison, a neat Stone Building, having but little of that look.

Here are three Watchmakers Shops; Mr *Peter Stretch* is the most eminent; next to him *John Wood*, then *Edmund Lewis*,[29] a brisk young Quaker, a Lover of *Supernaculum*.[30] They have two Fairs in the Years, when all Sorts of Household Furniture and Toys are sold. No Saints Days nor other Holidays are observed, except the First of *November*, the King's Birth-day and *Christmas Day*, by the Church People.

The Key for landing Goods is large and convenient, with Wharfs and Warehouses, stor'd with plenty of *European* Commodities, here being always at least 40 Ships of good Burthen in the River, and many are built after the *English* Fashion, the Woods producing Timber for that Purpose.

In the Summer time, People seldom wear Wigs, but thin Caps under

24. Andrew Hamilton (1676–1741), lawyer and Speaker of the Assembly, originally called himself Trent when he arrived in America. The reason for his change of name and the secrecy concerning his earlier life is unknown, although one rumor was that he had killed a lord in a duel. His estate, Bush Hill, was located just outside Philadelphia. See J. Thomas Scharf and Thomas Westcott, *History of Philadelphia, 1609–1884*, 3 vols. (Philadelphia: Everts, 1884), 2:1501–2.

25. Israel Pemberton (1684–1754) was a wealthy Quaker merchant (ibid., 2:1251).

26. Andrew Bradford (1686–1742) published the first newspaper in Pennsylvania, the *American Weekly Mercury*. See Anna Janney DeArmond, *Andrew Bradford, Colonial Journalist* (Newark: University of Delaware Press, 1949).

27. Society Hill received its name from the Free Society of Traders, an early corporation that by 1723 had ceased operations.

28. The Schuylkill River is slightly more than two miles west of Society Hill.

29. Both Peter Stretch (1670–1746) and John Wood (Sr.) (d. 1761) were established clockmakers with shops on Front Street in Philadelphia; both also had sons who would become accomplished Philadelphia clockmakers. See James W. Gibbs, *Pennsylvania Clocks and Watches: Antique Timepieces and Their Makers* (University Park: The Pennsylvania State University Press, 1984), 69–73, 79–81. Edmund Lewis left few traces in the city's records; perhaps he was the Edmund Lewis who apprenticed as a clockmaker in London for seven years in 1727 but who never completed his apprenticeship (see Atkins, *Register of Apprentices*, 180). Lewis presented a removal certificate from the New York monthly Meeting of Friends, recorded in Philadelphia on March 25, 1732 (Abstracts of Minutes, Philadelphia Monthly Meeting, vol. 3: 1730–85, p. 14, GSP).

30. A liquor to be drunk to the last drop, hence, alcohol of good quality.

their Hats, and without Coats, frequently going to Church without them. The Negroes and bought Servants, are clad in coarse Osnabrigs,[31] both Coat, Waistcoat, Breeches, and Shirt, being of the same Piece, and so rough, that the Shirt occasions great Uneasiness to the Body. This Wearing generally costs from fifteen to twenty Pence a Yard.

Four Miles from *Philadelphia* lies *German Town*,[32] so call'd because built and inhabited by the *Palatines*. It is a large Place, well contrived. These People are supposed to be 40,000 in *Pensilvania* only,[33] and behave themselves so well, as gains them the Respect of the *English*; and are ready, in case of an Invasion, to appear in the Defence of the Province, and frequently exercise themselves at their Arms. They have many considerable Farms, which they improve to the best Advantage: Many of them are naturaliz'd by Law, which enables them to purchase Lands, and capacitates them to hold Places in the Government. Since the first Settling of these People, not one of them have suffered the Law for any Offence.

During my Stay here, I had an Opportunity of conversing with a *Spanish* Gentleman who related to me his Adventures, which for their Singularity, I shall relate in his own Words.

31. A cheap, coarse, strong linen originally made in Oznabrug, Germany, and commonly worn by the lower classes in England and America (Peter F. Copeland, *Working Dress in Colonial and Revolutionary America* [Westport, Conn.: Greenwood Press, 1977], 204). See Figure 16 for a drawing of the type of clothing worn by slaves.

32. Germantown had a population of 340 in 1734 (Stephanie G. Wolf, *Urban Village: Population, Community, and Family Structure in Germantown, Pennsylvania, 1683–1800* [Princeton: Princeton University Press, 1976], 43).

33. About 52,000 people lived in Pennsylvania in 1730, while an additional 9,000 lived in Delaware, which was then under the jurisdiction of Pennsylvania (U.S. Bureau of the Census, *Historical Statistics of the United States, Colonial Times to 1970*, 2 vols. [Washington, D.C.: Department of Commerce, Bureau of the Census, 1976], 2:1168). The colony contained approximately 23,000 Germans in 1727, and about 2,300 arrived in Philadelphia's port between 1727 and 1730 (Marianne Wokeck, "The Flow and Composition of German Immigration to Philadelphia, 1727–1775," *PMHB* 105 [1981]: 259–60).

MY Name is *Alonso Tellez de Almenara*, of *Sevile*, Capital of *Andalousia*, in *Spain*, where I had a competent Fortune left me by my Father, which I considerably improved by trading to *Mexico*; but marrying unhappily, I became involved in Debt: The best Part of my Estate was sold for the Discharge of them; and with the Remainder I was resolved to seek my Fortune. After I had maturely considered to what Place I should go, I pitched upon *Hispaniola*. I agreed with *Don Silvia de Mendora* for my Passage. He was Commander of the *Esperance*, a Man of War of 50 Guns. I was a Voluntier. We sailed from *Cadiz* in 1710.

Three Days after we discover'd a Sail, and presently perceived, it was a Corsair of *Barbary*: Upon which the Captain called all Hands upon Deck, and prepared to give them a vigorous Reception. On their nearer Approach, we found them to be of superior Force to us; but being resolved to defend ourselves to the last, rather than submit to *Barbarian* Slavery, the Corsair began with us by a Broadside, which we returned, fighting it out with unparallell'd Bravery. But most of our Men being killed in the Engagement, we were obliged to strike to them, after an Hour and a half's Conflict; when they boarded us, and proceeded to rummage our Ship. I lost my Cargo consisting of about Eight Thousand Pieces of Eight, and all my Wearing Apparel. The Captain was plundered to the Value of 40,000 Pieces of Eight.

No sooner was the Hurry over, but all the valuable Effects were removed on board the Corsair, with myself and the remainder of the Crew, being only five Persons, the Slain, being nine in Number, were thrown over board. We were secured under Hatches, and the Ship steered its Course for *Sallee*,[1] a Piratical Port in the *Atlantick* Ocean, where we arrived in five Days. After some time we were set on Shore, in order to be presented to the King of *Morocco*, all Slaves brought into his Ports, being his Property.

After a short Stay, during which we were put into a Dungeon under Ground, by the *Moors* called *Mazmarra's*, we were conducted by Land towards *Miquenez*,[2] chief City of that Prince's Dominions, at about 36 Miles distance from *Sallee*; in the Kingdom of *Fez*.[3]

At our first Arrival we were presented every one of us with a Chain of twenty three Pounds Weight, which was fastened about our legs, and then were put into one of these Dungeons spoken of before, where was no Light, nor any Thing to sit upon. Our Food was *Cous Cous*, a Hasty Pudding made of Corn and Water.

After three Days Imprisonment, we were led out to be presented to the King, who about Eleven in the Morning, attended by about six hundred Blacks of his Guard, came to view the Works he was raising adjoining to his Pallace. He carefully examined our Physognomy, and observing one of us who seemed to be fearful, spoke to him in the *Moorish* Tongue, and demanded of him, if he would change his Religion, and become *Moor*. The Man answer'd in *Spanish*, he was resolved to die in the Religion of the Christians; which brave Speech so irritated this Prince, that, without speaking one Word more, he darted his Javelin at him, and struck him dead at his Feet. We all trembling, expected the same Fate.

After this Execution, he ordered us to be led to the Works. We

---

1. Located on the Atlantic coast of Morocco, Salé was a noted center for the corsairs.

2. During the late seventeenth century the Moroccan sultan used 30,000 workers, including at least 2,000 Christian captives, to construct the city of Meknes. See Ellen G. Friedman, *Spanish Captives in North Africa in the Early Modern Age* (Madison: University of Wisconsin Press, 1983), 67.

3. Fez was a town located in the interior of Morocco, approximately 125 miles east of Salé.

thought ourselves happy in escaping; so we were forced to climb up Ladders and Scaffolds loaden with Mortar and Timber besides our Chains, that before Evening we were so wearied, as is impossible to express: After Sun set we were conducted to our Prison. This Life I lived for one Year, in which time I have been Witness to above a Thousand Murders committed by this Inhuman Prince.

About this Time he meditated a War against the King of *Algiers*,[4] which Kingdom he fancied he might very easily add to his own, and passed the River *Meluya*, the *Mulucha* of *Sallust*, which divides the Kingdom of *Fez* from that of *Algiers*, with 60,000 Men, raw and undiciplin'd, mostly armed with Clubs and Javelins. I was in the Expedition. We marched towards *Tremezen*, a City not far from Mount *Atlas*, formerly Head of a Kingdom of the same Name, of about two Hundred Miles in Length, now added to *Algier*, which, with some Part of *Tunis* added, makes *Algier* the largest of the Kingdoms of *Barbary*.

We arrived at *Tremezen* six Days after our Setting out, but the *Algerines* were before us with 12,000 Men, Veteran Troops, who, without giving us time to put ourselves in Order of Battle, attacked us so vigorously, as compelled us to leave the Field, with 5000 Men killed, and 2000 made Prisoners. The Alcade that commanded was obliged to retire, and repass the River *Meluya*, and lost his Head for his Mismanagement.

I was soon after recommended to the King's Favour, and preferred to the Post of Receiver of the Taxes in the Province of *Tremezen*, so was freed from my Chain. I had an Opportunity of observing the Country, which is a fine one; but the Natives not having any Property, all being the King's, the Land lies uncultivated. From my first Advancement I formed several Projects to escape, but the Attempt being dangerous, I was cautious how I proceeded, and continu'd quiet two Years, when a Quantity of Gold being in my Custody, which I collected for the King's Use, I secured about forty Pounds Weight, with which I was resolved to leave the Place, when I had the least to fear.

On the twenty first Day of July, 1713, accompanied by a *French* Slave, I set out in the Night for *Ceuta*.[5] We travell'd all Night, and in the Day concealed ourselves in the Woods and Desarts, for fear of

---

4. A city-state east of Morocco.

5. On the northwest tip of Africa, Ceuta had been controlled by the Spanish for more than a century.

Lyons, Leopards, and other Beasts of Prey; and, to prevent discovery by the *Moors* and *Arabs*, we carefully avoided the Adours or Villages, and frequently saw the *Carracans*, but always had the good Luck not to be seen.

After five Nights ranging about, having no Guide but a Pocket Compass, we discovered in the Morning the Steeples of *Ceuta*, and the *Moorish* Army before the Town. We were sadly perplexed how we should pass the Camp, when suddenly the *Spaniards* made a Sally, and attacked the *Moors* so bravely, that they fled with the utmost Percipitation. The *Spaniards* pursued them, with so much Eagerness, that they left the Town two Leagues, and in coming back, a Party of them discovered us, and brought us into the Town, where we were congratulated upon our Deliverance. This Town is always blocked up by the *Moors*, by which Means they drive a Trade with the *Europeans*, for Guns and Gun-powder.

After I had remained with the Garrison sometime, I went on board a *French* Ship bound to *Malaga*; from whence I rode to *Seville*, and made myself known to my Friends, and was reconciled to my Wife, who in my Absence had, by the Wine Trade, acquired about 6000 Livres. I lived some Years with her in Love and Unity, after which she died, which threw me into a Melancholy; but it wearing off, I was resolved once more to settle in the *West Indies*, and sailed on board a Man of War to that Intent.

Our Voyage was prosperous, and we reached the appointed Place, which was St *Augustine* in *Florida*: But finding I was mistaken as to the Advantages I at first proposed, sailed for *Mexico*, but the Wind proving treacherous, by stress of Weather, we were drove upon the Coasts of the *English* Settlements, and anchor'd in *Chisapeak Bay*; where being informed of the Advantages I might meet from the generous Inhabitants, I went to *Philadelphia*, where I have lived many Years, and have, by Trade, acquired above one hundred thousand Pounds. I married an *English* Woman of Fortune, who is now living here: By her I have had some Children; I have an Opportunity of conversing with the Protestants of all Denominations, and comparing their Manners with the Catholicks, publickly renounced the Errors of the *Romish* Church and embraced that of the Church of *England*, in which I am resolved to continue.

5   BURLINGTON—CHURCHES AND
MISSIONARIES—QUAKER MEETINGS—THE MAYOR
OF PHILADELPHIA—RESCUING A
LADY—AN EXCHANGE OF WIT—A NEGRO'S
GHOST—THE DELAWARE RIVER—PERRIWIG
ISLAND—AN ENORMOUS
SKELETON—ANTEDILUVIAN REMAINS.

I left *Philadelphia*, to go to *Burlington* to my Master; I went in a Boat, where I got my self Drunk for the first time after my Arrival, and then first experienced the Strength of Rum. About Twelve we landed there, and I was conveyed to my Master, where I dined upon Dumplings, boil'd Beef, and Udder; when I became enamour'd with Mrs *Sarah*,[1] the Daughter. I was stripp'd of my Rags, and received in lieu of them a torn Shirt, and an old Coat. They tell me, it was only for the present, for I might expect better.

I went to bed that Night, being the first Time I had seen one since I left *London*, which was fifteen Weeks. The next day I had leave, upon

1. The title "Mrs" indicates Sarah Pearson's superior social station as the daughter of Moraley's master, not her marital status. Sarah Pearson would wed Joseph Hollinshead, who apprenticed under her father, in 1740. Hollinshead became Isaac Pearson's partner immediately after the marriage and inherited the clockmaking business when Pearson died. Hollinshead is mentioned in Williams, *Silversmiths of New Jersey*, 39–41; see also William Wade Hinshaw, *Encyclopedia of American Quaker Genealogy*, 9 vols. (Richmond, Ind.: Edwards, 1938), 2:249.

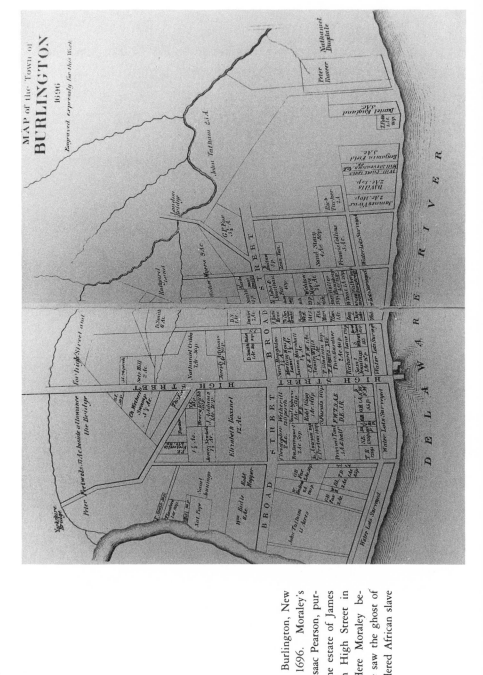

Map 3. Burlington, New Jersey, 1696. Moraley's master, Isaac Pearson, purchased the estate of James Wills on High Street in 1715. Here Moraley believed he saw the ghost of the murdered African slave in 1730.

Figure 12.   Friends' Meeting House, Burlington, New Jersey, 1683.

Figure 13.   Old St. Mary's Church, Burlington, New Jersey. Built in 1702.

my Desire, to walk about the Town: It is close to the River, and contains about 300 Houses; the Number of inhabitants was 800. It has a Key and Wharf, where Ships of 500 Tun may anchor: At the Upper-End, is the Prison, built of Brick.[2] Every House has a Garden and Orchard, stored with Apples, Peaches, and Cherries. Cyder is the common Drink here; some Houses making one hundred and fifty Barrels in the Year.

There are two Quaker Meetings, and one Church, which is of Brick, with a low Steeple; it is neat, and well contrived: The Incumbent, when I was there, was the Rev. Mr *Wayman*, a *Welshman*, a Gentleman of Parts, and the most extensive Goodness.[3] Since I have mentioned him, I think it necessary to say something of the State of the Church in these Parts. All the *British* Colonies are in the Diocess of *London*, and consequently the Bishop of that Place is Superintendant in Ecclesiastical Cases, who sends Missionaries to keep up a Vissibility of the Christian Faith, and to instruct the Natives; but I believe little Pains is taken with them.

The Sallaries settled on them as Missionaries, is fifty Pounds *English* yearly, and sent them in Vendible Goods, and brings them, by a right Management, £300 *per Cent*. This with the Cheapness of Provisions, enables the Clergy to keep up a good Figure, and frees them from Contempt. The Perquisites of their Profession brings them but little, because their *Easter* Offerings are but indifferently paid; and the other Branch of their Business, Matrimony, is disputed with them by the Magistrates, who marry as well as they. The Reason, I conceive, is, because of the great Distance of the Parishes, which makes it very chargable, and inconvenient in travelling, when a Justice can answer the End as well.

---

2. Located about twenty miles from Philadelphia, Burlington may have been even smaller than Moraley believed (see Map 3). Another contemporary indicated that "Burlington is situate on the River *Delaware*, is the Capital Town of that Division, called *West-Jersey*, containing above 200 families: the Place honoured with the Courts being kept here, the Houses were neatly built of Brick, and the Markets well supplied with Provisions." David Humphreys, *An Historical Account of the Incorporated Society for the Propagation of the Gospel in Foreign Parts* (London: Downing, 1730), 182. Nearly two decades later Peter Kalm observed that Burlington did not rival Philadelphia as a port town (Kalm, *America of 1750*, 1:321). Its importance continued to decline through the century. According to one report in 1780, Burlington contained only 160 houses and a total population of 1,110 (E. M. Woodward and John F. Hageman, *History of Burlington and Mercer Counties, New Jersey* [Philadelphia: Everts & Peck, 1883], 163).

3. The Reverend Robert Wayman served as rector of St. Mary's Church in Burlington (Figure 13) from 1730 to 1737.

Figure 14.   Clock from the shop of Isaac Pearson, William Moraley's master.

On the other Side of the River lies *Bristol*, in *Bucks* County, in *Pensilvania*, larger than *Burlington*; but has little remarkable in it, but is the Post Road to *Philadelphia*. I had almost forgot to speak something of the Quakers yearly Meetings, which I should have done in my Description of *Philadelphia*, or *Burlington*. They meet yearly at one of these Places alternately, by Agreement, when all Sorts of the best Provisions are provided for the Reception of great Numbers of the Brethren assembled from all Quarters, who are sometimes so numerous, that there is not room for them; which obliges them to disperse into the adjacent Villages for Quarter, but return in the Day to the Town.

At these times they dispense their Charity to the Poor and Needy, without any regard to particular Sect or Party: I have partaken of their Benevolence. Their stay is from *Saturday* Night, when they first arrive, till about *Wednesday*; when they reward the Servants where they reside liberally, and usually leave Money in the Family, for the Use of the

Poor, which is given at their Discretion. These Meetings are for the rebuking of Schisms, that sometimes arise among them; and to inquire into the external Behaviour of the Professors, and to preserve Unanimity. In a word, they shew to Mankind, that they are strict Observe[r]s of good Nature and Hospitality, and keep up to the due Observance of the Evangelical Precepts, and the Moral Law.

My Master employed me in his Business: I continued satisfied with him for sometime; but being desirous to settle at *Philadelphia*, during the rest of my Servitude, I declared to him, I would stay no longer, and desired him to dispose of me to some other Master, and insisted upon it, agreeably to the Tenour of my Indenture. This Demand made him cross to me, and I attempted an Escape, but was taken, and put into Prison; but was soon released, with a promise to satisfy my Demand. About a Fortnight after, we went to the Mayor of *Philadelphia*, his Name was *Griffith*,[4] a Man of exact Justice, tho' an *Irishman*, who reconciled us; so I returned back to *Burlington*, and continued with him three Years, he forgiving me the other Two: I was ever after perfectly pleased with my Master's Behaviour to me, which was generous.

There lived in the Family a Relation of his, named *Hannah Lambert*, a Gentlewoman of Beauty, good Parts, and a good Fortune, Daughter to Mr *Thomas Lambert*, a Native of *Yorkshire*.[5] One Day as this Lady and myself was crossing [the] *Delaware*, in a Canoe, it overset; so being in Danger, I forgot my own for her Safety, and taking her round the Small of the Waist, with one Arm, swam by the help of the other to the other Side of the River. She so sensibly remembered this Service, that all the Time of my stay in this Family, I never wanted Money. Her Father gave me five Pounds, and when ever I went into the Country, I generally made his House my resting Place, where I was very civilly treated.

Our Family consisted of a Wife and two Daughters, with a Nephew, a Negro Slave, a bought Servant,[6] and myself, with the aforesaid Gen-

4. Thomas Griffitts served as Philadelphia's mayor from October 7, 1729, to October 6, 1731, and from October 2, 1733, to October 1, 1734.

5. Thomas Lambert arrived from Yorkshire, England, on the ship *Shield* in 1678 and resided in Nottingham Township, New Jersey (W.J.P. [*sic*], "Major-General John Lambert," in "Notes and Queries," *PMHB* 12 [1888]: 191). He died in 1733, according to a report in the *American Weekly Mercury*, March 20–27, 1733. When Hannah Lambert married Dr. Thomas Cadwalader in 1738, her wealth enticed him to give up his Philadelphia practice, move to her residence in Trenton, and take over the administration of her very valuable estate; they subsequently had seven children (William Henry Rawle, "Col. Lambert Cadwalader: A Sketch," *PMHB* 10 [1886]: 2–3).

6. The "bought Servant" was Aaron Middleton (see Figure 17).

tlewoman. We had a next Door Neighbour, called *William Cullum*,[7] a *Lincolnshire* Man, and a Baker: He came to us one Day, as my master and myself were making Nails for a Bellows for a Forge; and laying down upon the Bellows Board Three-pence and Sugar, writ the following Words in Chalk, and left the Place, we not knowing from whence the money came.

> *Here's Money, Sugar, fetch some Rum,*
> *And when the Liquors made, I come.*

My Master perceiving it, said, Well, this is *William Cullum's*, in order to shew his Wit, and order'd me to answer it Extempore. I first fetched the Rum, then made the Liquor, which was *Bombo*, and writ under the foregoing Lines.

> *The Liquor's made, besure to come,*
> *Or send more Sugar, and more Rum.*

Which my Friend perceived, laughed, and gave me a Shilling, with which I merrily quaffed.

One Night as I was in Bed with my Fellow Servant, being awake, the Chamber Door opened without any Noise, and I perceiv'd something coming cross the Floor, like a Ghost, in White, with a black Face. The Sight was so terrifying, that I shrunk under the Bed Cloaths, and sweated heartily, and endeavoured to wake my Friend, but to no Purpose. It came to the Bedside, and stooping, grined, and stared me in the Face, and beckened with its Hand: At which I shiver'd so much, and my Chops chatter'd, as if beating a March; but recollecting myself, I demanded of it what it wanted. Then it beckoned again, and left the Room; but soon after came again, looked earnestly at me. When I said, *Lord! why do you come here?* It answer'd, *Nothing with you*, as I well remember, and then went away, the Door shooting after it, without any Noise. I was very positive it was a Spirit, and told the Family the next Morning; who said, it was a Negro killed some Years since by her Master, and that they had often seen it.[8]

The [Delaware] River is supposed to have its Rise from a Lake, in the

7. A baker in Burlington, William Collum died in 1740 or 1741, leaving his property to his wife, Mary. Isaac Pearson's will in 1748 mentioned Mary Collum as a neighbor living on High Street. (Wills, 2:105, 373.)

8. See Appendix G for the 1686 case of the murder of a slave in Moraley's residence in Burlington.

Mountains of *Canada*, and is believed from its first Spring to the *Capes*, in its Windings, to be above 2000 Miles in length.[9] In the Heat of Summer, nothing affords a more pleasant and delightful Prospect than it does. On both Sides are to be seen handsome Houses, surrounded with great Numbers of Gardens and Orchards, blessed with great Variety of Fruits, salutiferous Plants and Herbs. Along the Banks are found divers Sorts of curious Shells, which are carefully gather'd and sent as Rareties to *Europe*. Great Numbers of large Sturgeon gamble on the Water, often times leaping quite out. The Boys in a Summer's Evening swim, but keep near the Shore, for fear of the Sharks. The Navigation extends above 200 Miles; but at a Town called *Trent Town*, twenty Miles from *Philadelphia*, no Ship or Boat can pass, by reason of a Chain of Rocks cross the River from Side to Side.[10]

In the Month of *July*, in 1731, one *Lawrence Houlton*,[11] and myself, being Fishing in a Canoe, a Water Snake, of about six Foot long, offer'd to board us: We had much ado to prevent him. He jumped several Times, but we beat him of[f] with our Fishing Sticks. About half an Hour after, we discover'd a bald Eagle, hovering in the Air, who descended often, and at last seized a lame wild Goose, swimming on the Water, and carried it off. These Birds live chiefly upon Fish, and on that Account are generally found near the Rivers; they often have Battles in the Air with the Hawks, but are always beaten.

Along the Banks of this River are many trading Towns, with convenient Docks and Keys, where are landed Goods, for the mutual support of each other, such as Wood for Firing, Rum, Sugar, Molasses; likewise coarse Linen, of which there are some small Manufactures, tolerably good. Fish is so plentiful, I have seen large Boats and Barges, loaden to the Brim with them, such as Roach,[12] Pearch, and Trouts, larger than those caught in *England*.

9. The Delaware River actually originates in the Catskill Mountains of New York and runs about 370 miles to the Delaware Bay. The bay extends for an additional 50 miles before emptying into the Atlantic Ocean.

10. Trenton is 116 nautical miles, and Philadelphia 80 nautical miles, from the Atlantic Ocean by way of the Delaware Bay and River.

11. Lawrence Houlton (Holstin, Holstein, Holson, or Holston) lived in Pilesgrove, Salem County, New Jersey, from at least 1715 until his death in 1750. He was not a wealthy man; his personal estate was valued at less than £9 at his death. (AIS; Wills, 2:244.)

12. According to Samuel Johnson, "a *roach* is a fish of no great reputation for his dainty taste: his spawn is accounted much better than any other part of him: he is accounted the water sheep, for his simplicity and foolishness; and it is noted, that *roaches* recover strength, and grow in a fortnight after spawning" (*Johnson's Dictionary*, 348).

On both Sides are many Creeks, as large as most of our Rivers, which being Navigable for small Vessels, are made use of to convey Necessaries to the Country People, from the larger and remote Country Towns. These Creeks are so deep, that no Bridges are to be met with to cross over, so Boats and Ferries are provided at certain Stages. The People generally chuse to live near these Creeks, which is the Reason the Country far from them is thinly inhabited.

In the midst of the River *Delaware*, are many small Islands, some of them two Miles in length, others half the length, which are fertile. In the Summer the Cows will swim to them, from either Shore, and graze till the Evening, when they will return, but sometimes with the Loss of a Leg, by the Shirks. I have been in some of these Islands. Here is one call'd *Perriwig Island*,[13] from its resembling one in its Shape: It is two Miles and a Half long, and lies seventeen Miles from *Burlington*, nothing has a more Romantick look than this Place: It is furnished with many Sorts of Fruits and Roots, especially wild Grapes, and of the Muskadel Kind, with Sassafras.

Caves are here so convenient, as if perfected by Art: in one of them the Bones of a Man were found, which if all the Rest were in the same Proportion, would form a Skelliton of near thirty Feet in length. I saw a Thigh Bone and a Tooth, which last would, in the Hollow of it, contain near half a Pint of any Liquid.

Farther up the Country are Copper Mines, producing Copper near as good as that of *Sweden*, which much inriches the Proprietors, and imploys great numbers.[14] Coal Mines have been discovered; but as Wood is Cheaper, it is not used. In many places are to be seen the remains of *Deucalion's*,[15] or *Noah's* Flood; such as the Figures of Fishes imprinted upon divers Sorts of Shells, with several Strata's of Earth; some with Shells, others with the Bones of Animals. Near *New York*, Cottages have been discovered buried under Ground above two hundred Feet deep.

I have inquired of the *Indians*, if they had any Account of Time

13. Shaped something like a periwig (a wig), Newbold Island is somewhat smaller than Moraley indicates, and it lies about seven miles upstream from the town of Burlington. Facing the island on the western shore of the river was Pennsbury.

14. In 1749 Peter Kalm noted the earlier economic importance of these New Jersey copper mines, although they had flooded by the time Kalm traveled through the area (Kalm, *America of 1750*, 2:621). The history of these Bergen County copper mines is in Wayne Bodle, "'Such a Noise in the World': Schuyler's Mine and the Response in the Middle Colonies, 1719–1729" (Paper presented at the Seminar of the Transformation of Philadelphia Project, University of Pennsylvania, March 20, 1989).

15. According to Greek mythology, Deucalion and his wife Pyrrha were the sole survivors of a flood sent by Zeus to destroy the human race.

among them, in order to trace out a History, to give Mankind some
Account of their Origine; but they assured me, they have no written
Tradition, nor any Memorial left them by their Forefathers, that can
give the least Satisfaction.

From the frequent discovery of human Bones, of such Magnitude as
are continually found, we may reasonably believe Men were formerly of
larger Stature than at present; and to make this appear the more proba-
ble, there have been discovered proportionable Caves for their Reception, above two hundred Feet under Ground; which makes it plain, that
the Race of large Men ended by the universal Flood: This Opinion is
believed by the *English* here, with whom I have discoursed concerning
these Matters.[16]

16. Colonial Americans commonly attributed large fossil bones to an earlier race of giant human
beings. See David Levin, "Giants in the Earth: Science and the Occult in Cotton Mather's Letters to the
Royal Society," *William and Mary Quarterly*, 3rd ser., 45 (1988): 751–70.

6   PLANTATIONS IN PENNSYLVANIA—
INDIAN CORN—"THE BEST POOR MAN'S
COUNTRY IN THE WORLD"—WILD BEASTS—RATTLE
SNAKES—HORN SNAKES—HUMMING BIRDS—LOCUSTS—
BUTTERFLIES—THE NEGROES—SLAVE
LAWS—BOUGHT SERVANTS.

BEFORE I observed, that I continued with my Master at *Burlington*, in perfect Concord. I acting as a Watchmaker, he often detached me into the Country to clean Clocks and Watches: It was in these Journeys I had an Opportunity of discovering what I have observed relating to the several Descriptions contained in this Book.

Almost every inhabitant, in the Country, have a Plantation, some two or more; there being no Land lett as in *England*,[1] where Gentlemen live on the Labour of the Farmer, to whom he grants a short Lease, which expiring, he is either raised in his Rent, or discharged his Farm. Here they improve their Lands themselves, with the Assistance both of bought Servants and Negroes. They raise *Indian* Corn, for the Subsis-

1. Although land ownership was more prevalent in the Middle Colonies than in England, Moraley's claim that land was not leased in the Mid-Atlantic region was certainly exaggerated. See, e.g., Lucy Simler, "The Landless Worker: An Index of Economic and Social Change in Chester County, Pennsylvania, 1750–1820," *PMHB* 114 (1990): 163–200.

tence of their Families, after this Method: The Ears of Corn of the last Years growth is sown in the Beginning of *April*; they dig a Trench in the Ground, about five Inches deep, into which they strew the Grains, a few at a Time, for fear they should Sprout out too thick, and cover them lightly with Earth. After six Weeks it shoots out, then the Planters rake with a Hough the Ground, round the Stalk, to strengthen it: This is done every six Weeks, till the Corn is confirmed, which is brought to perfection the Beginning of *September*, when they strip the Corn from the Stalks, which they convey to their Granaries, leaving the Stalks to rot, which fertilizes their Land. With this Corn they make a kind of hasty Pudding, boiling it in Salt and Water, till it is thick; then pour it into a Dish, and serve it up with Milk, sometimes with Butter, but most commonly with Treacle.[2] It is a hungry Food, and is called *Mush*, being not unlike a Dish called *Cous Cous*, used in the Kingdoms of *Fez* and *Morocco*. They make use of it for Puddings, both boiled and baked, which with Eggs, is as good as a Rice Pudding. Raisins and Currants are seldom used, by reason of their Dearness, being Twelve-pence a Pound.

This Country produces not only almost every Fruit, Herb, and Root, as grows in *Great Britain*, but divers Sorts unknown to us. Bread Corn is superior to ours for Whiteness, and Cheaper. Barley is not so good, tho' they make Beer of it: Our Ten Shilling Small Beer is infinitely preferrable to any brewed there. Butter is very good, but Eight-pence a Pound; so Fish is generally eaten with the Butter it is fried in, with a little Vinegar to make it sharp. Butchers Meat, particularly Pork, is cheaper and better than with us; being fed with *Indian* Corn and Acrons. I have seen the Planters shake the Peach Trees to the Hogs.[3]

The Country is every where diversify'd with Woods, and well manured Farms: And the hospitable Inhabitants dispence their Favours to the Traveller, the Poor and Needy. I have travelled some Hundreds of Miles at no Expense, Meat and Drink being bestowed upon all the subjects of *Great Britain*; for they strive to out-do one another in Works

2. Commonly eaten in England, treacle is a syrup produced during the refining of sugar.

3. Casting peaches before swine was one of the wonders of the Delaware Valley, and many visitors remarked on the incredible natural abundance implied by this practice. See, e.g., the comment made by Gabriel Thomas in 1689 in Albert Cook Myers, ed., *Narratives of Early Pennsylvania, West New Jersey, and Delaware, 1630–1707* (New York: Barnes & Noble, 1912), 324. And Peter Kalm noted that in Europe "hardly any people but the rich" could eat peaches, while in the middle colonies they were fodder for pigs (Kalm, *America of 1750*, 1:40–41).

of good Nature and Charity. In short, it is the best poor Man's Country in the World; and, I believe, if this was sufficiently known by the miserable Objects we have in our Streets, Multitudes would be induced to go thither. Journeymens Wages are Five Shillings a Day,[4] and is paid to Joiners, Carpenters, Bricklayers, and Barbers, &c.

The Rivers are well stored with Fish, as Roaches, Pearch, Trout, Cat Fish, which makes excellent Broth. Sturgeon I have bought one eight Foot long for Ten-pence; Flounders, Eels, Sun-Fish, Rock-Fish, better than our Cod; Oysters larger than *English* ones, and much better, the Shells are one Foot long. Here are Swans, Peacocks, Geese, Turkies, Ducks, Pidgeons, both Wild and Tame; Cocks and Hens are cheap, a fat Hen is sold for Two-pence Half-penny in the Markets; Pheasants, Partridges, Woodcocks, Quails, Plover, Snipes, besides small Birds unknown to us.

Here are Rabbits, but they are rather Hares, smaller than ours, they are seldom larger than *English* Rabbits, and the Flesh tasting like the Flesh of *English* Hares. Squirrels are of different Kinds, the smallest having Wings like a Bat, which helps them to fly from Tree to Tree. Panthers, Wolves, and Bears, are common; besides Horses, the hardiest in the World, for after a Riding of many Miles, being hot, they leave them standing in the Streets all Night, without catching Cold.

Otters, Badgers, Wild Cats, and a Beast called Scunck, who if you approach near them, will piss on their Tails, and switch them in your Face, and the Stink will continue above a Week. The Possum, which will retire to a tree when pursued, where hanging by its Tail, which it twists round the Branches, will defend itself against its Enemies, with the young in its Belly, which is a false one, for that use.

Here are Foxes, both Red, Grey, and White; besides Racoons, of the same Nature and Qualities, of whose Furs, worked up with Beaver, are made the best of Hats. Frogs are numerous, and of different Colours; their Legs are much longer than those of *Europe*; some are coloured like a Leopard, others streak'd like a Tyger with black and yellow Spots, which makes them of a frightful appearance. Here are no Toads; Lizards are of various Sorts and Colours, but not Poisonous; and are looked upon as Forerunners of Snakes, which are of many Sorts; as First,

The Rattle Snake, about six or seven Feet in Length, and so Poisonous, that if the Party bitten, does not cut off the Part bit, Death immediately ensues. The Natives have found out a Plant, which, if

4. Master craftsmen hired journeymen on a daily, weekly, or often longer basis.

presently applied to the Wound, perfects a Cure. The Discovery was made by the Indians thus; when a Snake has bitten either Man or Beast, he presently flies to seek out this Plant, and eats some of it, to prevent its poisoning its self; and it has been discover'd, when he has missed of this Plant, he has been found Dead: the Truth of this has been confirmed to me by several discreet Persons.

The Rattles do not begin to grow till the Snake is three Years old, then every Year one is produced: Whenever this Animal leaps at either Man or Beast, he first shakes his Tail, then rises half his Length. This seems to be a Contrivance of the good Providence of God, in order to prevent the direful Consequences from the bite of this noxious Creature. One *Joseph Rose*,[5] of *New Jersey*, shewed me a Set of Rattles, to the Number of 37 from one Snake; so the Age of it was 40 Years.[6]

The Horn Snake is the next Dangerous, about the same Length and Bigness, having a Horn at the Extremity of its Tail, through which there is a Concavity, where with he ejects his Poison. If by accident he strikes his Horn into a Tree, it dies in two Days time, and the Leaves wither, and fall to the Ground. This I thought incredible, but the Natives attested it to me for Truth; and is not to be wonder'd at, considering all Trees and Plants have contain'd in them a vegetable Life.

The Red Belly'd Snake is commonly in Length five or six Feet, he is very Poisonous. The Green Snake of the same Length and Qualities. The Water Snake large, and extreme hurtful. The Garter Snake harmless and beautiful. The Yellow or Wampum Snake, as hurtful as any. Two Sorts of Adders, or Vipers, hurtful, as large again as ours. Two Sorts of Black Snakes, so bold in Gendering time, that they will run after People and bite them, but not Venomous; they are six, seven, or eight Foot long.[7]

---

5. Two men named Joseph Rose appear in the surviving records. One was the Philadelphia printer who assumed the business of his father after his death in 1738 (*American Weekly Mercury*, June 28—July 4, 1738). Another Joseph Rose (1704–76) was born in Ireland and migrated to Philadelphia, arriving in the city on October 21, 1729. He moved to Burlington, where he eventually married a wealthy widow and then moved to Lancaster, Pennsylvania. He was admitted to the bar in 1750. See Charles I. Landis, "The Juliana Library Company in Lancaster," *PMHB* 43 (1919): 243.

6. Moraley's accounts of snakes are better read as local folk belief than as a naturalist's observations. Many of the superstitions and tall tales recounted by Moraley survived into the twentieth century. See Phares H. Hertzog, "Snakes and Snakelore of Pennsylvania," *Pennsylvania Folklife* 17 (1967): 14–17.

7. Peter Kalm also noted the excessive numbers, length, and aggressiveness of black snakes in the countryside surrounding Philadelphia (Kalm, *America of 1750*, 1:313–17).

Lastly Ground Snakes, about seven or eight Inches long, like our Hag
Worms.

These Animals in the Summer time frequent the Woods, which not
being much resorted to by Men, they increase in such Abundance, that
I believe, where we have One, here are five Thousand; one shall often
meet them sunning themselves, and in the Woods concealed under old
rotten Wood, and dried Leaves, where they have a secure Retreat. If any
accident befalls them, by being wounded, they live till the setting of
the Sun, then die. They subsist upon Frogs, and it is diverting to see
the fear the Frog is under at the approach of his Adversary. The Snake
pursuing, and the Frog leaping from him, till finding it in Vain to
resist his superior Enemy, leaps into his Jaws, who is sometime in Swallowing him, always beginning at his Legs.

The Humming Bird is very remarkable for his Smallness and Beauty;
his Body no larger than a Bee. He is so called for his Humming when
he flies. His Bill is long and straight, in Proportion, as a Woodcock's.
His Body beautifully adorned with Variety of Feathers of different Colours, Gold being the most perspicuous, and so fine, one would think
they were Down. He never alights on the Ground, but hovers, in the
Summer time, over the mellifluous Flowers, his proper Food; when, by
the Help of his Bill, he sucks out the Sweets, and retires to the Cherry
Tree, his natural abode, where he builds his Nest.

I have observed a Wasp to build his Nest over a Smith's Chimney, in
a very odd Manner. I was working at the Forge, when I espied a small
Chimney raised against the Wall of the Forge, near the Fire. It was
about six Inches long, made of wet Dirt, which the Animal brought in
its Mouth, about the Bigness of a Pea, and with its Feet plaster'd
against the Wall, beginning from the Bottom; and had first made a
Convex, in order to support the System, like an arched Door-way, or
Window, and raised the whole Fabrick in a Convex Form: At the Upper-end he laid his Nest.

Here is a Beetle, called by the Natives a Tumbleturd, which for the
Oddness of its Building its Nest, deserves a Description. About *April*,
both Male and Female, leave their old abiding Place, to find a more
proper one; which having done, find out a Hole about two Foot under
Ground, into which they descend, by a Crack made by the Heat of the
Sun, in order to make their Nest, then they leave the Place, and after
they have found a small Piece of wet Earth, the Bigness of a Pea, they

roll it along the Ground, it growing as it gathers the Dust, to the Place appointed, where they tumble it in, and lay their Eggs in the midst of the Ball, which is as large as a Coit,[8] where they are hatched by the Sun.

The Manner of rolling the Ball is thus: The Male sets his fore Feet against the Ball, and drives it forward. On the opposite Side the Female stands erect and with her fore Feet pulls it towards her. When either of them are tired, they do not forsake their Work, but change their Posts. Sometimes one of them being very weary with shoving with its Fore Legs, reverses itself, and standing upon its Fore Legs, shoves the Ball with its Hind Legs, the Head being downwards. If by any Accident one of them should be missing, the other does the whole Duty, by driving the Ball alone.

I have often, in observing these Creatures, reflected on the wonderful Effects of Nature, and admired the Infinite Wisdom of the Creator, who has embued the least of his Productions with a seeming Degree of Reason (if I may be allowed to term it so) in order to bring about his Divine Purposes. In this Part of the World, one has always an Opportunity of observing such a diversity of Wonders, as naturally raises in us a Co[n]templation of the abundant Goodness, Power and Mercy, of the Beneficent Creator.

The Mocking Bird, is another Animal, of an odd Nature: He is called so for his incessant Noise like the Barking of a Dog, and often occasions the unwary Traveller, to mistake his Way. I was once lost in the Woods by hearing one of them, and tracing out the Noise; sometimes it was before me, then behind, that I was five Hours before I could find the Way home.

About the same time appears another Bird call'd Whip for Will, from his Cry, being like the Expression of those Words: He usually begins to tune his Pipe about Nine in the Morning, sitting on a Branch of a Tree, not far from the Ground, and continues till the Setting of the Sun.

Here are Bald Eagles, having no Feathers, on their Heads: They hover over Rivers, and very frequently catch Fish, by suddenly darting on the Water. Here are also Hawks and Vultures, but for Linnets, Green Birds, Larks, Goldfinches, Bulfinches, and Chaffinches, here are none to be found. Bees are numerous, who leave their Honey in hollow Trees. Several People make a Living by seeking for it; and so plenty, that one

8. A Coit, or quoit, is a flattish ring of iron. In the eighteenth-century game of the same name, it was thrown at a pin stuck in the ground with the object of encircling the pin.

Hundred Pound Weight has been found in one Tree. Musketoes are troublesome in the Summer time; but the People make Fires before their Houses in the Evenings, which banishes them away.

Before I left *America* there was such a prodigious Flight of Pidgeons seen that almost darkened the Air, and infested the Fields and Villages, and so tame, that they became the Food of the Inhabitants for a Month together. They alighted in whole Flocks, and rested upon the Tops of Houses and Barns in a starving Condition, being by Necessity drove from some other Country. In 1732, in *July* and *September* an Insect called a Locust appeared, which was looked upon as a bad Omen, and it accordingly happened, for presently after, they came in such Swarms, that the Trees were covered with them, and devour'd the Leaves and Fruit: Their Bodies are about the bigness of the Humming Bird, having a black Head, and Eyes jutting out like black Beads. Their Colour is not unlike a Spanish Fly. About seven Years before this, a Swarm of Squirrels came over [the] *Delaware* River, and entered the Houses.

Here are Many Sorts of Butterflies, larger than those in *England*, so finely coloured, as causes in the Beholder both Wonder and Delight: They build their Nests in the Leaves of Cabbages, and continue their Abode in them, till their Young are brought to Perfection, then leave them to shift for themselves. So admirable are the Effects of the Divine Providence in supporting the most minute of his Productions, that makes me break out in the Words of *David, How manifold, O Lord! are all thy Works; in Wisdom hast thou created them.*[9]

At the first Peopling [of] these Colonies, there was a Necessity of employing a great Number of Hands, for the clearing the Land, being over-grown with Wood for some Hundred of Miles; to which Intent, the first Settlers not being sufficient of themselves to improve those Lands, were not only obliged to purchase a great Number of *English* Servants to assist them, to whom they granted great Immunities, and at the Expiration of their Servitude, Land was given to encourage them to continue there; but were likewise obliged to purchase Multitudes of Negro Slaves from *Africa*, by which Means they are become the richest Farmers in the World, paying no Rent, nor giving Wages either to purchased Servants or Negro Slaves; so that instead of finding the Planter Rack-rented, as the *English* Farmer, you will taste of their Liberality, they living in Affluence and Plenty.

"richest farmers in the world"

9. Psalms 104:24: "O Lord, how manifold are thy works! in wisdom hast thou made them all: the earth is full of thy riches."

Figure 15. Newspaper advertisement of slaves for sale, *American Weekly Mercury* (Philadelphia), June 8–15, 1738.

The Condition of the Negroes is very bad, by reason of the Severity of the Laws, there being no Laws made in Favour of these unhap[p]y Wretches: For the least Trespass, they undergo the severest Punishment; but their Masters make them some amends, by suffering them to marry, which makes them easier, and often prevents their running away. The Consequence of their marrying is this, all their Posterity are Slaves without Redemption; and it is in vain to attempt an Escape, tho' they often endeavour it; for the Laws against them are so severe, that being caught after running away, they are unmercifully whipped; and if they die under the Discipline, their Masters suffer no Punishment, there being no Law against murdering them.[10] So if one Man kills another's Slave, he is only obliged to pay his Value to the Master, besides Damages that may accrue for the Loss of him in his Business.

The Masters generally allow them a Piece of Ground, with Materials for improving it. The Time of working for themselves, is *Sundays*, when

10. New Jersey's slave law of 1716 required citizens to whip both slaves coming into the colony without permission and resident bondspeople discovered five miles from their master's home without a written pass. Courts could order unlimited corporal punishment of slaves who attacked people "possessing Christianity"—that is, whites. See James C. Connolly, "Slavery in Colonial New Jersey and the Causes Operating Against Its Extension," *Proceedings of the New Jersey Historical Society* 14 (1929): 194–99.

Figure 16.   Runaway slave, 1730. William
Moore of Chester County, Pennsylvania, described his fugitive slave, Jack, as wearing
"a new ozenburg Shirt, a pair of strip'd
home-spun Breeches, a strip'd ticking
Wastecoat, an old dimity Coat of his Master's with Buttons of Horse teeth set in
Brass, and Cloth Sleeves, a felt Hat almost
new."

they raise on their own Account divers Sorts of Corn and Grain, and sell
it in the Markets. They buy with the Money Cloaths for themselves and
Wives; as for the Children, they belong to the Wives Master, who bring
them up; so the Negro need fear no Expense, his Business being to get
them for his Master's use, who is as tender of them as his own Children.
On *Sundays* in the evening they converse with their Wives, and drink
Rum, or Bumbo, and smoak Tobacco, and the next Morning return to
their Master's Labour.

They are seldom made free, for fear of being burthensome to the
Provinces, there being a Law, that no Master shall manumise them,
unless he gives Security they shall not be thrown upon the Province, by
settling Land on them for their Support.[11]

11. Masters were legally obligated to post a bond of £200 when manumitting a slave, and they
could be required to support their former bondspeople if they became a burden on the community. Such

Their Marriages are diverting; for when the Day is appointed for the Solemnization, Notice is given to all the Negroes and their Wives to be ready. The Masters of the new Couple provide handsomely for the Entertainment of the Company. The Inhabitants generally grace the Nuptials with their Presence, when all Sorts of the best Provisions are to be met with. They chuse some *Englishman* to read the Marriage Ceremony out of the Common Prayer Book; after which they sing and dance and drink till they get drunk. Then a Negro goes about the Company and collects Money for the Use of the Person who marry'd them, which is laid out in a Handkerchief, and presented to him.

This is the only free Day they have, except Sundays, throughout the whole Course of their Lives, for then they banish from them all Thoughts of the Wretchedness of their Condition. The Day being over, they return to their Slavery. I have often heard them say, they did not think God made them Slaves, any more than other Men, and wondered that Christians, especially *Englishmen*, should use them so barbarously. But there is a Necessity of using them hardly, being of an obdurate, stubborn Disposition; and when they have it in their Power to rebel, are extremely cruel.[12]

The Condition of bought Servants is very hard, notwithstanding their indentures are made in *England*, wherein it is expressly stipulated, that they shall have, at their Arrival, all the Necessaries specified in those Indentures, to be given 'em by their future Masters, such as Clothes, Meat, and Drink; yet upon Complaint made to a Magistrate against the Master for Nonperformance, the Master is generally heard before the Servant, and it is ten to one if he does not get his Licks for his Pains, as I have experienced upon the like Occassion, to my Cost.

If they endeavor to escape, which is next to impossible, there being a Reward for taking up any Person who travels without a Pass, which is extended all over the *British* Colonies, their Masters immediately issue

---

laws naturally discouraged the manumission of slaves. Free African Americans in New Jersey were subject to a variety of social and legal restrictions—for example, they could have only a life interest in property rather than own it in fee simple, and therefore they could not leave real estate to their families because it escheated to the Crown on their death. See Connolly, "Slavery in Colonial New Jersey," 194–99.

12. Moraley may have heard about the first major organized slave revolt in British North America, which occurred in New York in 1712; authorities put eighteen slaves to death after the revolt. See Kenneth Scott, "The Slave Insurrection in New York in 1712," *New-York Historical Quarterly* 45 (1961): 43–74; and J. Davis, *A Rumor of Revolt: The Great Negro Plot in Colonial New York* (New York: Pantheon, 1985).

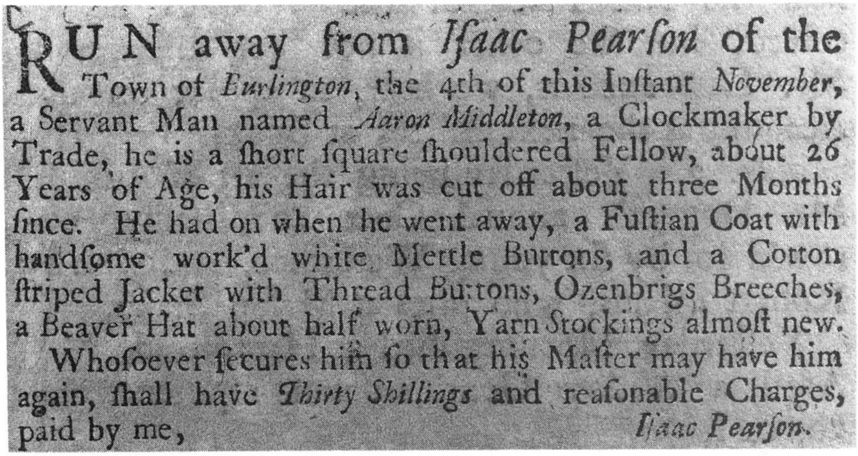

RUN away from *Iſaac Pearſon* of the Town of *Burlington*, the 4th of this Inſtant *November*, a Servant Man named *Aaron Middleton*, a Clockmaker by Trade, he is a ſhort ſquare ſhouldered Fellow, about 26 Years of Age, his Hair was cut off about three Months ſince. He had on when he went away, a Fuſtian Coat with handſome work'd white Mettle Buttons, and a Cotton ſtriped Jacket with Thread Buttons, Ozenbrigs Breeches, a Beaver Hat about half worn, Yarn Stockings almoſt new. Whoſoever ſecures him ſo that his Maſter may have him again, ſhall have *Thirty Shillings* and reaſonable Charges, paid by me,   *Iſaac Pearſon*.

Figure 17. Newspaper advertisement for runaway servant of Isaac Pearson, *American Weekly Mercury* (Philadelphia), November 2–9, 1732.

out a Reward for the apprehending them, from Thirty Shillings to Five Pound, as they think proper, and this generally brings them back again. Printed and Written Advertisements are also set up against the Trees and publick Places in the Town, besides those in the News-papers. Notwithstanding these Difficulties, they are perpetually running away, but seldom escape; for a hot Pursuit being made, brings them back, when a Justice settles the Expences, and the Servant is oblig'd to serve a longer time.[13]

13. By New Jersey law, escaped servants were to serve two extra days for each day they were absent, and the courts could add additional time to compensate masters for expenses incurred in capturing runaways (Abbot Emerson Smith, *Colonists in Bondage: White Servitude and Convict Labor in America, 1607–1776* [Chapel Hill: University of North Carolina Press, 1947], 267). Figure 17 reproduces a newspaper advertisement for a servant who absconded from Moraley's master.

7 THE INDIANS IN PENNSYLVANIA—THEIR
HABITS, MANNERS, AND RELIGION—COLONIAL
CURRENCY—THE GOVERNOR AND HIS
COUNCIL—THE FAMILY OF WILLIAM PENN—
CHARITY OF THE QUAKERS—DRINKS—FISH AND
FRUIT—THE CLIMATE—"THE TENNIS
BALL OF FORTUNE."

THE Native Inhabitants are the *Indians*, who are a civiliz'd, hand-
some-limb'd People: None amongst them were ever born deform'd or
crook'd.[1] Their Complexion is of a Copper Colour; with broad flat Faces,
thick Lips and Noses. The Men are generally tall and slender, but the
Women are short and fat. Their Habit, both Men and Women, is much
alike, since their Acquaintance with the *English*, most of them wearing
a Match Coat, made of coarse *Scotch* Plaid, the Breeches and Stockings of

1. The Europeans called the people living along the Delaware Bay by the name of "Delaware."
These Unami-speaking people, more correctly called the Lenape, inhabited what is now New Jersey and
parts of Pennsylvania, Delaware, and New York. Of course, Moraley's description of their health is
exaggerated. His views are in accord with the somewhat romanticized notions adopted by many Europeans as the Native American population declined along the eastern seaboard and no longer posed a
substantial threat to the white invaders. See Herbert C. Kraft, *The Lenape: Archaeology, History, and
Ethnography* (Newark: New Jersey Historical Society, 1986), xvii–xviii; and Peter O. Wacker, *Land and
People: A Cultural Geography of Preindustrial New Jersey: Origins and Settlement Patterns* (New Brunswick,
N.J.: Rutgers University Press, 1975), 57–60, 104–5.

the same, with Cotton stuff'd in their Ears, and Brass Thimbles hanging at them. But the Kings have Belts of Wampum, which is their Money, hanging about their Necks.[2]

They hunt Deer for their Living, and other Kinds of Beasts, both wild and tame.[3] The King[4] first receive[s] his Tribute out of the Profits arising from their hunting, then they sell the Remainder to the *English* for Sugar, Molasses, Guns, Gun-powder, and Rum. With the last they make themselves drunk; and when all is spent, return home. I have met them in the Fields in their Return, sitting in a Ring, so drunk, that they could not stir from the Place.

In the Succession of their Kings they observe an Hereditary Right, the Son always taking his Father's Place. These People pay them a Respect suitable to their Dignity; though their Grandeur is not much superior to that of their Subjects, only differing from them in living idle, and upon their Tribute, which is not very great. Their Dominions are not above forty Miles in Circumference, wherein are no Towns, but dispers'd Wigwams, or low Houses.

There is always a perfect Agreement subsists between the *English* and them, for generally every two Years, or three at furthest, they visit the Governors of the Provinces, attended by near two thousand of their Subjects, in order to renew the ancient Friendship between them.[5] As soon as Notice is given of their Approach, the Governor sets out to meet them, attended by the principal Inhabitants, and pays them extraordinary Honours, treating them and their Followers several Days together. After this they enter into Treaty with one another, which is either to ratify and confirm the ancient Ones, or make new Ones. Then they return Home, loaded with Presents and Drink.

They are so just in the due Observance of these Treaties that there is not one Instance of Breach of Covenant can be brought against them.

2. Wampum consisted of cylindrical beads made from the ends of polished shells threaded on strings; these served as the currency among many Native Americans and in their early dealings with Europeans (Kraft, *The Lenape*, 202–7).

3. Most Lenape engaged in a mixed economy, depending on agriculture, hunting, gathering, and fishing for their livelihood. By 1730 some Lenape were able to carry on their traditional way of life, although others in the area grew increasingly dependent on agriculture as hunting became less viable. See ibid., 225; Wacker, *Land and People*, 60–68.

4. A chief, usually referred to as a "king" or "sachem" by Europeans, headed each Lenape band and exercised considerable influence although not unlimited power (Wacker, *Land and People*, 58).

5. Although the Quakers in West Jersey generally lived peacefully with the Lenape, Moraley overstates the harmony between the races. By 1730 relatively few Lenape still lived in the area, which clearly helped minimize conflict. (Ibid., 84–88.)

These Agreements are chiefly relating to Violences that have or may be committed by the Subjects on either Side; and if a Murder is committed by an *Indian* upon an *English* Subject, they will send out Parties and pursue the Murderer till they have found him, and then deliver up the Offender to Justice. But if an *Englishman* Murder an *Indian*, and the *English* refuse to deliver him up to Justice, they will come in great Bodies and demand him, to be punish'd by them. But of late it is agreed to punish each Offender where they find him; so if the *Indians* find a Subject of *England* guilty of Murder, they punish him with Death, though the Offence was committed against an *Englishman*. In the same Manner the *English* proceed against an *Indian*; by which means all Acts of Hostility are prevented.

As to their notions of Religion, they are very wild, having none establish'd among them; but believe there is a God, Creator of all Things, endowed with Wisdom, Goodness, and Mercy; and believe they shall be judged, punished, and rewarded, according as they observe the moral Precepts instilled into them by the Light of Nature, and the Tradition of their Fathers.[6]

Their Arms for War were formerly Bows and Arrows; but since their Communication with the *English*, they use Fire Arms. If they are engaged in War, which seldom is amongst themselves, but against the Neighbouring *Indians*, the Vanquished are sure to suffer from the insulting Victor, by burning or scalping the Skin and Hair from their Heads, in the Presence of the King, and their whole Nation, assembled for that Purpose.

They live in little Huts, called Wigwams, so low, that without stooping and creeping upon all Fours they cannot get into them.[7] As the *English* purchase Lands of them, they retire farther Westward from our Settlements.[8] Hunting is allowed to them and all others, there being no Lords of Manors to hamper them with their Privileges;[9] and here are

6. The spiritual beliefs of the Lenape were much more complex than Moraley portrays. See Kraft, *The Lenape*, 161–94.

7. The Lenape actually lived in a variety of structures, including wigwams and longhouses (ibid., 104–27, 214–15; Wacker, *Land and People*, 61).

8. By the time Moraley passed through the area, most of the Native Americans, demoralized by military defeat, the devastation of European diseases, and the continual growth and expansion of the white population, had sold or abandoned their lands and withdrawn westward, primarily to western Pennsylvania. See Kraft, *The Lenape*, 224–36; Wacker, *Land and People*, 84–88; and Daniel K. Richter, "A Framework for Pennsylvania Indian History," *Pennsylvania History* 57 (1990): 246–47.

9. The Pennsylvania custom of allowing hunting on unimproved private land was considered so important that it was written into the Pennsylvania Constitution of 1776 (Theodore Thayer, *Pennsylva-*

plenty of all Sorts of Venison, both cheap and good, and larger than ours.

Money is very scarce, being carried from Province to Province, from whence it never returns; so they are obliged to emit more new every three Years. *English* Money is the most valuable, one Guinea passing for Twenty-eight Shillings,[10] every Shilling for Eighteen-pence, Six-pence for Nine-pence, one Half-penny for a Penny; but as there are not enough to supply the Exigence of the State, both Paper and Parchment Money passes for current Coin, by the Authority of the Governor and Assembly; a Petition being lodged with the Governor, setting forth, That the Money is either defaced, or dispersed into the other Provinces; so that there is a Necessity of new Emissions, perhaps to the Value of 40 or 50,000 Pound.[11]

The Governor takes time to consider if their Allegation is true, and advises with his Council if it be convenient to grant them their Request; when after a mature Deliberation, he commonly gives his Consent, for which he receives a Premium, paid him first out of the new Coin, of about 2000 Pounds, and acquaints the Lords Commissioners of Trade and Plantations with the Affair, for their Approbation. Then Presses are set up, and the Money is coined, and deposited in the Loan Office, where Persons under Difficulties pawn their Lands, for such sums as they have Occasion for, and pay Interest. With this Interest the Proper Officers Sallaries are paid, and the Remainder serves to defray the Expenses of the State.

The Value of this Money is from one Shilling to five Pound, canton'd into Bills of one, two Shillings and Six-pence, three, five, six, ten, fifteen, twenty Shillings, three Pound, and five Pound Bills, of about four Inches long, and three Inches in breadth; and on divers Places are expressed the Value, with the Arms of every Province, and the Names of Persons who sign them, deputed by the Governor, to prevent Counterfeits.

The Governor of *Pennsilvania* has a salary of 2000 Pounds a Year

nia Politics and the Growth of Democracy, 1740–1776 [Harrisburg: Pennsylvania Historical and Museum Commission, 1953], 225).

10. A guinea was worth 21 shillings in England.

11. The assembly issued £30,000 Pennsylvania currency in 1729 and an additional £40,000 in 1731. In a pamphlet in 1729, Benjamin Franklin advocated a liberal paper-money policy (Leonard W. Labaree, ed., *The Papers of Benjamin Franklin*, 28 vols. [New Haven: Yale University Press, 1959–], 1:141).

allowed him, and receives five hundred Pounds a Year from the Independent Counties of *Newcastle, Kent*, and *Sussex*, where he presides in the Assembly, at certain Times in the Year.[12] This is the *Civil List*, and he has it granted from Year to Year, which is confirm'd to him every Session. He is nominated by the Heirs of the late *William Penn*, but confirmed by the King, and is seldom removed. His Perquisites arise from a Poll Tax, of Four Shillings in the Pound, from all single Persons that have been resident in the Province one Year; married Men pay only Two Shillings. He likewise receives Eight Shillings and Four-pence, for every Marriage License.

The Governor's Council consists of the most substantial Persons as to Figure and Fortune, and are to him the same as a House of Lords. The Commons are deputed from the Towns and Counties, and the Members, to qualify them to sit, must have either 1,000 Acres of Land, or fifteen hundred Pounds in Money. In their Proceedings, they endeavour to imitate the same Method as is used in the *British* Parliament; and here are Persons of Ingenuity and polite Literature. The Magistrates are not obliged to be of the Established Church, to qualify them to enjoy Posts of Honour and Profit. Here they discharge the Duties of their several Trusts, without regard to Difference of Religion or Party; both Quaker and Churchman living together in perfect Harmony.[13]

The Family of *Penn* have very great Respect paid them by all Sorts of Persons, tho' they have no share in the Administration of the Government Affairs. They received, when I was there, about 14,000 Pounds *per Annum*, for Quit Rent, as an acknowledgment to them as Propri-

---

12. Patrick Gordon served as deputy governor of Pennsylvania from 1726 to 1736. Moraley probably overstates the governor's salary, because Governor Evans (1703–9) estimated his annual income as only £300. William Penn acquired title to the three "lower" counties (now Delaware) in 1682 from the Duke of York. See Jean R. Soderlund, Richard S. Dunn, and Mary Maples Dunn, eds., *William Penn and the Founding of Pennsylvania 1680–1684: A Documentary History* (Philadelphia: University of Pennsylvania Press, 1983), 8; and Winfred Trexler Root, *The Relations of Pennsylvania with the British Government, 1696–1765* (1912; reprint, New York: AMS Press, 1969), 57.

13. Moraley exaggerates the suffrage and office-holding requirements in Pennsylvania and New Jersey. In colonial Pennsylvania, any male Christian who was at least twenty-one years old, two years resident in the province, and the owner of fifty acres (including twelve cleared) or £50 in property could vote and hold office. The governor's council was not the equivalent of the House of Lords, since it had no legislative functions and was confined to being an advisory body. See Thayer, *Pennsylvania Politics*, 4–6. In New Jersey, voting and office-holding requirements were less clearly stated and were sometimes subject to political maneuvering. However, the 1705 law stipulated that all freeholders could vote and that those who had £500 sterling in personal property were also eligible for membership in the House. See John E. Pomfret, *Colonial New Jersey: A History* (New York: Scribner's, 1973), 126.

etors, at about Five Shillings every hundred Acres. They have a fine Seat at *Pennsbury*, eight Miles from *Philadelphia*, near the River, but it is now in a ruinous Condition. It has a large Orchard, stored with Apples and Peach Trees. The Family built this House in One Thousand Six Hundred and Eighty Two. I was there in 1731.

This Province was settled upon them, on Account of a Debt due to Admiral *Penn*,[14] in consideration of Services done by him to the Government, till the Debt was discharged, and was granted by Charter from *Charles* the Second.[15] The present Proprietor is *Thomas Penn*, Esq., a worthy good-natur'd Gentlemen.[16]

The Laws here are the same as in *England*, as a Basis; but they have introduced so many By-ones, for the particular Government of Towns, as they pretend, for the more speedy Execution of Justice, that in some Cases destroys the Liberty of the Subject; nothing being more common than to see Men committed to Prison without legal Warrant, by the arbitrary Authority of the Magistrates.[17] I have been twice committed in this Manner, but one good Thing is to be observed, there being no vexatious Suits commenced upon frivolous Quarrels, which drains the Pockets of the lowest Class of Men in *England*: For upon the Appearance of a Quarrel, the Neighbours meet, in order to make an amicable Agreement, which being put to Arbitration, reconciles the Parties.

In the Towns as well as Country they are civil to all Strangers; and if they behave themselves well, will encourage them to stay among them, and marry. What induces many to stay, is the Cheapness of Provisions, and the Women, who are very handsome. Besides many have good Fortunes, perhaps Fifteen or Twenty Thousand Pounds.

The Quakers have a Custom of raising Money at their several Meet-

---

14. Admiral William Penn (1621–70) was the father of William Penn, founder of Pennsylvania.

15. Charles II granted the large tract of land to William Penn on March 4, 1681, partly in lieu of the £16,000 debt owed to Penn's father's estate (Soderlund et al., *William Penn*, 3; Joseph J. Kelly Jr., *Pennsylvania: The Colonial Years, 1681–1776* [Garden City, N.Y.: Doubleday, 1980], 17).

16. Thomas Penn (1702–75) was the son of William Penn.

17. The Pennsylvania criminal code concerning felonies was disallowed in 1718 and replaced by a law requiring the death penalty in accordance with English practice. Misdemeanors and the civil law were not affected by this change, so at times Pennsylvania and British practice diverged. See Alexander James Dallas, *Laws of the Commonwealth of Pennsylvania, from the Fourteenth Day of October, 1700*, 4 vols. (Philadelphia: Hall & Sellers, 1796), 1:133. John Murrin argues that American court procedures did not become Anglified until the late colonial period (John M. Murrin, "The Legal Transformation: The Bench and Bar of Eighteenth-Century Massachusetts," in Stanley N. Katz and John M. Murrin, eds., *Colonial America: Essays in Politics and Social Development*, 3rd ed. [New York: Knopf, 1983]). Of course, suspected runaway servants, slaves, and apprentices could be arrested by any sheriff. Although arrest warrants probably should have been issued, they were frequently neglected.

ings, as I observ'd before, with which they do many charitable Offices to the Poor and Indigent. I have experienc'd the Effects of their Benevolence. If any Person, though a Stranger, continues to do well, by preserving a good Character, and they have a good Opinion of them, they will enquire into his Circumstances, and if it appears he is distress'd in his Business for want of Stock, or necessary Implements to carry on his Trade, they will set him up out of this Money, without demanding any Security either by Bond or Promissory Note; and if he repays them, they will never give him any Trouble.

Their Marriages are very chargeable, many times the Wife's Fortune being expended at the Celebration of the Nuptials.[18] The Town Folks are generally invited to them, when all Kinds of Rarities are consum'd. Their Burials too are attended by all Sorts of People, both Whites and Blacks; and Hot Wine and Sugar Cakes[19] are dispers'd among them. I have partook of their Liberality on these Occasions. It is given to all Persons standing in the Streets, and sitting at their Doors. Their Ways of House-keeping are not much different from ours.

Cyder is the most plentiful here of all Liquors; besides which they have Mead, Methlegin, Perry, and Peach Drink.[20] The Beer [is] not good. *Madeira* Wine[21] is the only Wine us'd here. Rum is sold for Three-pence the Half-pint, or Ten-pence a Quart. Half a Pint of Rum being mix'd with three Half-pints of Water or Small Beer, makes *Bombo*; but mix'd with Cyder, makes *Sampson*, an intoxicating Liquor.

The Markets in all the Towns are well stor'd with all Sorts of Provisions, cheaper than at *Newcastle upon Tyne*. Fish is so plentiful, that large Pearch and Roach are sold for Three-pence a Dozen, and Trouts at the same Price. 'Tis dangerous fishing for them for the Water Snakes, one being forc'd to wade up to the Knees in the Runs where they are most plentiful. One day one *John Houghton*[22] of *Burlington* and myself, being distress'd for a *Sunday*'s Dinner, went a fishing and in twenty Minutes caught between us 140 Perch and Roach; and in returning home to his

---

18. Marriage ceremonies among Quakers in colonial America often were quite elaborate and costly. See J. William Frost, *The Quaker Family in Colonial America: A Portrait of the Society of Friends* (New York: St. Martin's Press, 1973), 174.

19. Sugar cakes are a sweetened or flavored bread.

20. All are alcoholic beverages. Mead and methlegin were made from a mixture of honey and water, and perry was fermented from the juice of pears.

21. A wine produced on the island of Madeira, located about four hundred miles from the northwest coast of Africa.

22. The Houghton family resided on the south side of High Street in Burlington; John Houghton lived in Hopewell Township, Burlington County, in 1741 (AIS).

Father's, to get 'em dress'd, we sold five Dozen of them for Fifteen-pence, and the Remainder serv'd six People for Dinner. The Money was laid out in Rum and Sugar, to wash them down. These sort of Fish are generally 10 or 12 Inches long.

The Country is generally level, but woody, having but few moun-taneous Parts, (they lying more Westward, where are no Inhabitants) and produces many sorts of Trees, as Hiccory, Oak, which together make the best and most durable Firing; Sassafras, White and Red Cedar, Ash, Pines, Limes; abundance of Grapes, both of the Red and Muscadel Kind; plenty of wild Peaches, but sour. The Garden Peach grows upon standing Trees as large as Apple Trees. I have seen eleven Sorts, but the Early Peach is best. The next in Goodness is the Plumb Peach. Mulberries are of two Sorts, Black and White, but not near so good as the *English* ones, and are much smaller. Morello and Black Cherries[23] are very good and cheap, so are all the other Sorts.

Here are Currants and Rasberries, Strawberries, Blackberries, with Artichokes and Asparagus, Collyflowers, Turnips, Parsnips, Beans and Peas, as good as any in *England*; Potatoes, *Jerusalem* Artichokes, Pome-granates, Muskmellons, and Yams, better than Potatoes; also *Indian* Corn, which boil'd young, and eaten with Butter, is as good as Chest-nuts, having almost the very same Taste.

In the Summer time, which begins to appear about the First of *May*, the long Winter on a sudden disappears, and the mellifluous Flowers and Plants, with their fragrant Smell, gratify the Senses with a wonder-ful Diversity, and the melodious Songsters of the Woods, the Fields and Groves, chant forth their Joy in warbling Notes, forming even a terres-trial Paradise. Then a clear Sky, and constant refreshing Breezes, revive the glad Planter, and he no more remembers the cold Winter's pinching Frost, but chearfully cultivates his teeming Soil, expecting from his Labour a grateful Return for his Industry.

This Country, were it not for the Uncertainty of the windy Weather, which often disappoints the industrious Planter, would be one of the noblest in the Universe; but the North East Wind that generally blows for near three Quarters of the Year, is the Occasion of it. One hot Day is succeeded by a cold one, which checks and pinches the Fruits of the Earth, and often retards their Growth.

During the Summer, which lasts but three Months, the Sun burns

23. Morello is a cherry with a bitter taste, and black cherries usually are wild cherries.

and parches the Earth, which opening, receives the descending Rain, and fertilizes it. The Soil in many Places is like Garden Ground, being from three to five Foot deep of Black Mould, which Fatness produces great Quantities of all Sorts of Corn and Grain.[24] In the Year 1730, eight Persons dropp'd down dead in one Day, at *Philadelphia*, by reason of the excessive Heat of the Weather.[25] It is dangerous to drink Water at this Season, hot Liquor being more proper, to allay the Thirst.

Then Thunder and Lightning, with terrible Gusts of Wind and Rain, descend, and surprise the Inhabitants. The first Beginning is, a violent Storm of Wind arises, obliging the People to secure their Windows, to prevent their being shatter'd. It then blows so hard, as often lifts the People off the Ground. Then succeeds a violent Rain, which continues but for about ten Minutes; then Thunder and Lightning, which clarifies the Air. After which appears a Serenity in the Sky seldom seen in *England*. Then the green Fields and verdant Meadows display their several Beauties, advantageous to the joyful Shepherd.

Every where are to be found pleasant useful Rivulets of salubrious Water, and the larger streams over-flow the adjacent Meadows, rendering them prolifick.—Thus has the benign Creator display'd his Power and Goodness in the Production of all his Works.

The Winters are so severly cold as benumbs the Inhabitants, and begins so early, that from the Fourth of *November* to the Twenty-fifth of *March*, in 1730, the great River *Delaware* was hard frozen, Coaches and Carts passing it on either Side.[26] One *Andrew Galloway*[27] an *Irishman*, and myself, going over in a Sled, the Ice broke, and he was drown'd.

The Cold was so excessive, that the People were obliged to keep [in]

---

24. New Jersey actually contained extremely variable soils, although the area surrounding Burlington was among the best in the colony (Wacker, *Land and People*, 10–12).

25. The month of July 1734 was the hottest in this period; five people were reported to have died of the heat (John F. Watson, *Annals of Philadelphia, and Pennsylvania, in the Olden Time*, 3 vols. [Philadelphia: Stuart, 1899], 2:353).

26. Europeans frequently remarked on the cold weather in the Mid-Atlantic region and noted that the Delaware River often iced during the winter months (e.g., Kalm, *America of 1750*, 2:677–78). The winter of 1733–34 was one of the coldest in the eighteenth century. The Delaware River did not begin to thaw until mid-February, and it was not navigable until the second week in March. See David M. Ludlum, *Early American Winters, 1604–1820* (Boston: American Meteorological Society, 1966), 47–48; Samuel Hazard, "Effects of Climate on the Navigation of the River Delaware, 1681–1828," *Hazard's Register of Pennsylvania* 2 (1828): 23; and reports from the *New England Weekly Journal* (Boston), March 19, 1734.

27. Andrew Galloway appeared among the many debtors listed in the inventory of Enoch Fenton, butcher, of Burlington in 1732 (Wills, 2:173).

their Houses; and all Business was at a stand. Divers Persons lost the Use of their Limbs for some Days, during the Sharpness of the Frost, it being more than ordinary Cold. I was forced to carry Wood for Firing, was pinched to such a Degree, that I thought myself unhappy in living. I often reflected on the Prodigal Son, and wished with him to eat the Husks that were given the Swine in his Father's House.[28]

During my stay in these Parts of the World, I have experienced the Mutability and Inconstancy of human Affairs; for from a tollerable State of Life, I have been reduced to Poverty, then have been up-set, then down: In short, I have been the Tennis-ball of Fortune,[29] and may say, with *Hudibrass*,[30]

> *I that was once as great as* Caesar,
> *Am now reduced to* Nebuchadnezzar:
> *Like as a Dog that turns a Spit,*
> *Bestirs himself, and plies his Feet,*
> *To climb the Wheel; but all in vain,*
> *His own Weight brings him down again.*
> *But still he's in the self same Place,*
> *Where at his setting out he was.*

But I being of a Temper not easily cast down by Adversity, continue, though down, and wait for a Trump Card to repay me what I had lost.

---

28. The story of the prodigal son is from Luke 15:11–32.

29. John Webster expressed similar popular sentiments in "The Duchess of Malfi" in 1614: "We are merely the stars' tennis-balls, struck and bandied / Which way please them" (Esther Cloudman Dunn, ed., *Eight Famous Elizabethan Plays* [New York: Modern Library, 1950], 537).

30. *Hudibras* is Samuel Butler's seventeenth-century verse-satire on Puritanism. Moraley accurately quotes the initial two lines of the canto entitled "An Heroical Epistle of Hudibras to His Lady." The balance of Moraley's poem, with its shift from a regal to a homely metaphor, is not from *Hudibras* and may well be an original conceit by Moraley. The awkward rhyme scheme (spit/feet, vain/again, place/was) would tend to rule out a more proficient poet as the author. See Samuel Butler, *Hudibras, in Three Parts, Written in the Time of the Late Wars {1678}* (Baltimore: Lucas & Nicklin, 1812), 304.

Indenture ends, "released"
"became free"

8   END OF SERVITUDE IN PENNSYLVANIA—"A ROVING TARTER"—COURTING ADVENTURE—TRENT TOWN AND BURLINGTON—ENCOUNTER WITH A PANTHER—DETAINED FOR A RUNAWAY—JOURNEY TO NEW YORK—AN INDIAN KING—THE GOVERNOR OF NEW YORK—PURSUED BY CREDITORS.

MY Master, after we were reconcil'd, behav'd very civilly to me, and I liv'd very happy, to the Expiration of my Servitude. He had a Share in an Iron Work at a Place call'd *Mount Holly*,[1] about seven Miles from *Burlington*, where I was sent to Work. Here I have had many a merry Day. Sometimes I have acted the Blacksmith; at other times, I have work'd in the Water, stark naked, among Water Snakes. Sometimes I was a Cow Hunter in the Woods, and sometimes I got Drunk for Joy that my Work was ended.

At last this Iron Work was perfected and the Time of my Servitude expir'd, and I became free. 'Tis impossible to express the Satisfaction I found at being releas'd from the precarious Humour and Dependence of

---

1. Isaac Pearson, Mahlon Stacy, and John Burr purchased 345 acres of land in 1730 and built a furnace and forge at Mount Holly on the south branch of Rancocas Creek (Boyer, *Early Forges and Furnaces*, 128ff.). It was a relatively isolated place, and only 281 people lived in the rural township including Mount Holly in 1709 (John Rodgers, "Census of Northampton, Burlington County, 1709," *Proceedings of the New Jersey Historical Society* 4 [1849]: 33–36).

my Master. He accouter'd me in an indifferent Manner, and gave me
my Discharge, to find out a new Way of Living.[2] I then went to *Philadelphia* and served one *Edmund Lewis*, a brisk young Clock-maker; but he
being unsettled, and of a roving Temper (*like Master, like Man!*), I left
him, and liv'd with Mr *Graham*, a Watch-maker, newly arriv'd, and
Nephew to the famous Mr *Graham* in *Fleet-street*.[3] With him I continued
ten Weeks, at Ten Shillings *per* Week Wages, and my Board found me;[4]
but he designing to settle at *Antegoa*,[5] I left him.

Then I roam'd about like a Roving *Tartar*,[6] for the Convenience of
Grazing, and for three Weeks had no Abiding Place. In the Nights I
was forc'd to skulk about the Extremity of the Town, where I lay in a
Hay-loft. In the Day time, I got Victuals of several of my Companions
from *London*. Then, by their Help, I courted an old ugly Maid, who had
got good store of Pewter and Brass.[7] The Match was agreed, and a Day
appointed to put me in possession of her Moveables:[8] But the very
Night before the Marriage was to be celebrated, she gave me a Gold
Ring to take the Bruises out,[9] and accidentally meeting with some of
my Acquaintance, they got the Ring from me, sold it, and spent the
Money; so I lost my Sweet-heart.

But this Life not being likely to last long, and the People's Good-
nature beginning to cool, I set my Wits to Work how to get home. But

instability

2. That is, Moraley received inexpensive clothing as part of the "freedom dues" when his period of
servitude expired.

3. William Graham, nephew of George Graham, was present in Philadelphia circa 1733; see John
Edwards, *The Complete Checklist of American Clock and Watchmakers, 1640–1950* (Stratford, Conn.: New
England Publishing, 1977), 19. A Fellow of the Royal Society and author of many scientific papers,
George Graham (1673–1751) was a famous watchmaker and inventor. His shop stood at the Dial and
One Crown in Fleet Street, London. See G. H. Baillie, C. Clutton, and C. A. Ilbert, *Britten's Old Clocks
and Watches and Their Makers* (New York: Dutton, 1956), 278–80.

4. Food was provided as part of the wages.

5. Antigua, an island in the West Indies.

6. A strolling vagabond.

7. The woman may have been Elizabeth Paris, a recent widow and a brass founder. She advertised
for a runaway apprentice in the June 11, 1730, issue of the *Pennsylvania Gazette* and died in the summer
of 1741 (*Pennsylvania Gazette*, August 27, 1741).

8. That is, to wed, for once Moraley was married he legally would have owned his wife's property.

9. Gold rings blessed by a priest on Good Friday, and sometimes inscribed with Bible verses, were
given as gifts and used for betrothals. These "cramp-rings" were believed to have the power to cure
various maladies. See John R. Gillis, *For Better, for Worse: British Marriages, 1600 to the Present* (New
York: Oxford University Press, 1985), 62; and W. Carew Hazlitt, *Faiths and Folklore of the British Isles:
A Descriptive and Historical Dictionary*, 2 vols. (1903; reprint, New York: Benjamin Blom, 1965),
1:154.

not presently hearing of a Ship bound for *England*, I was reduc'd to such Extremity, that I look'd like the Picture of bad Luck, and so thin, that you might have seen my Ribs through my Skin, and I was greatly afraid of a Consumption.[10] However, having some Acquaintance in the Country, I went about cleaning Clocks and Watches, and follow'd the Occupation of a Tinker;[11] but not being well vers'd in that Trade, where I mended one Hole, I was sure to make another.

But this Life serving only for the present, did not afford me a constant Supply; so in the Intervals was forc'd to spend, when I came back, what I had earn'd in these sort of Roamings. It never cost me any Money, by way of Expense; I was welcome every where, though unknown, and always recommended to Business from Place to Place, where I had Variety of Entertainment, always endeavouring to ingratiate myself into the People's Favour by a modest and decent Behaviour, which, with relating Stories when desir'd, and my giving them an Account of *England*, gain'd me the Reputation of an intelligent Man, though upon Occasion I could rake with the best of them, and change my Note as proper Time offer'd.

I remember I was going to a Place call'd *Cross-field*, between *Trent Town* and *Burlington*,[12] to mend a Clock, being bare-foot and barelegg'd; and after I had acquitted myself in the best Manner, and receiv'd Ten Shillings for my Pains, I went to *Trent Town*, a pretty neat Place, containing about 200 Houses, and lay there two Nights, after I had clean'd two Clocks. This Town stands twenty Miles from *Burlington*, near the River *Delaware*, having many handsome Houses, and rich Inhabitants.

Here I found out the young Lady whom I sav'd from drowning, who, by the Death of her Father, was left possess'd of a Fortune of Three Thousand Pounds.[13] She ask'd me to take a Dinner with her, which I did, and after that drank Tea with her, when she gave me Three Pound, and desir'd to know how Things stood with me; which having satisfied her in, I took my Leave of her, in order to return home.

10. A "consumption" described a number of different diseases that wasted the body. Often the disease was pulmonary tuberculosis.

11. An artisan who mends pots, kettles, and other household utensils made from tin, a base metal not used by watchmakers.

12. Moraley probably means the town of Crosswicks, between Burlington and Trenton (see Map 2).

13. Hannah Lambert was the daughter of Thomas Lambert. When he died in 1733, she shared his estate valued at nearly £5,000 (not including real estate) with her three sisters (Wills, 2:42–43).

About four Miles from *Trent Town*, passing along a spacious Road, I espy'd a Beast at a Distance, and observ'd his Eyes were fix'd upon me. I was so terribly affrighted, that, to prevent any Danger, I climb'd up a large Oak Tree and secur'd myself in the Branches. When the Beast drew near, I perceiv'd that it was a Panther, about the Largeness of a Mastiff Dog. He set his Fore Feet against the Tree, and attempted to climb up. I was so terrified at this, that I shiver'd, and all my Passions were at Work: But after he had tried to ascend in vain, by falling down twice, he roar'd, and gently left the Place.

It was near two Hours before I ventur'd to descend, for fear he should have conceal'd himself, in order to surprise me; and when I did venture down, I walk'd so warily, that it was near two Hours more before I reach'd the next House, which was but two Miles from the Place. This prov'd to be the Habitation of Mr *Isaac Horner*,[14] a *Yorkshire* Gentleman of Substance. I told him of this Adventure, at which he laugh'd, and said he had been in the same Circumstances. After Mr *Horner* had treated me with the best his House afforded, I went to Bed. In the morning I set out for home, but miss'd my Way.

Here are so many Cross Roads, which makes it exceeding difficult to keep the Right one; for instead of taking the Right, I struck into a broad Road, which, I was afterwards told, leads to a Wood of Pines, that grow close together, over-shadows the Road, and prevents any Communication with the Sky. In these Woods, Bears, Wolves, and Panthers range about, often putting the Traveller into a Fear. If I had continued this Way, I should not have met with a House till I came to *Salem*, a Town near the *Capes*, which was near two hundred Miles from me.[15]

After I had journied about eight Miles in the Road, not finding any Appearance of any House or Farm to enquire of, and fearing the Consequence of being lost in the Woods, I returned, happily for me, and guessed at a Road, which led me to *Allons Town*, a pitiful dirty Hole; where I arrived after nine Hours Travel, not meeting with any one to direct me. I drank some Cyder, eat some Hung Beef, and got Directions to *Recklish Town*, seated on the River, eight Miles from *Trent Town*,

14. Isaac Horner lived in Burlington County between 1704 and 1739 (AIS).

15. Moraley was indeed lost, because Salem is not on the land route to the Capes, although the town would be passed when one was sailing down the Delaware River. The Capes are about 100 miles from Trenton; Allentown, New Jersey, lies southeast of Trenton (see Map 2). Recklesstown is now Chesterfield, New Jersey.

where I was known. Here I came and was received well. It is a pretty large neat Place, of about Fifty Houses.

From thence I took the Right Road, and lost it, which so perplexed me, and being dispirited I broke out into the following Expressions, *If ever I have the good Fortune to reach my Native Country, I am resolved to reform my Life and Conversation, in such a Manner, as not to suffer a sinful Thought to harbour in my Breast.* Night coming on, I was in a sad Taking, reflected on my former Condition of Life, and, comparing it with the present, said, *I that was brought up so tenderly by my indulgent Parents, am now reduced to the most deplorable Circumstances.* *woe .*

Thus ruminating with myself, at last I discovered a Light at a great Distance, and endeavour'd to make up to it. After some Difficulty I got to it, and it proved to be the Habitation of *John Montgomery*, a *Scotchman*, where I was taken up for a Runaway, and detain'd all Night.[16] However I got a good Supper, consisting of hot Wheaten Bread and Milk, and a hot Apple Pye. In the Morning I was carried on a Horse by two Men to *Burlington*, where my former master cleared me, by producing my Indentures; and the Men returned home, but with this difference, that they had their Labour for their Pains, and Money out of Pocket upon my Account.

Three Days after this Adventure, I worked Journey Work with *Peter Bishop*,[17] a Blacksmith, for eight Shillings a Week, and Necessaries found me, as Lodging, Meat and Drink. I worked at the great Hammer, in making Horse Shoes, Horseshoe Nails, rounding of Ship Bolts, sharpening Coulters[18] for the Plow, &c. This Life I followed six Week, and out of my Earnings bought a fine shirt, the first I wore since my Departure from *England*. Many a hard Day I have had at this Employment, but necessity enabled me to surmount all Difficulties.

During this employ, my Creditors at *Philadelphia*, where I owed trifling Debts, such as Three or Four Shillings to each, but amounted in the Whole to above Eight Pound, found me out, and threaten'd me with summoning me before the Magistrate. This obliged me to leave my Blacksmith, for at that Time I could never hear a Dun with Pa-

16. John Montgomerie (d. 1733), a resident of Burlington County, had recently served as governor of New York and New Jersey (Wills, 2:342).

17. Peter Bishop, blacksmith, appears in many Burlington records. Thomas Wetherill, apparently Bishop's father-in-law, resided in Burlington City at his death in 1759 and owned property in several counties in New Jersey (Wills, 3:354).

18. A plow's iron blade, which cuts through the soil.

tience; so I steer'd my Course for *New York*, to avoid their Imperti-
nence. After three Days march, I arrived at *Elizabeth Town*, about eighteen Miles from *New York*. Near which Place, as I was walking in the
Road, I espy'd a new Brick House, and a Negro working in an adjoining Field, who called to me, and asked me if I would not come and see
his Master, who was an *Indian* King.

Little Persuasion serv'd, being weary; so I went with him, and was
admitted to the Royal Presence. The King was sitting by the Fire Side,
upon a Carpet, attended by two bought Servants, and Three Negro
Slaves, drinking Rum. His name was *Yo-Taen-San-Lo*, King of the *Chi-
apase*. After paying him a Respect due to his Quality, he desired me to
sit down and smoak a Pipe, and order'd Pipes and Tobacco to be
brought; and Rum, a Glass of which being handed to me, I soon dis-
patched it. He kindly ask'd me if I was an *Englishman*. I told him, I
was, and born at *London*. Then he drank to me again, and I pledg'd him
a second Time. He invited me to Dinner, and a Quarter of Lamb was
roasted.

After Dinner Punch was set upon the Carpet, when we drank heartily. Then he desired me to relate to him the Manners and Customs of
the *English*, with the State of our King; which I did, wonderfully magnifying every Thing, and making our King ten Times greater than he
is. After drinking three or four Glasses more, I would have taken my
Leave of him, but he desired me to stay an Hour longer, which I did;
and then took notice of his Furniture, which was good Chairs and
Stools, provided for Strangers, for they never use any themselves, nor
Beds.

At last I got leave to depart, and made the best of my Way to *New
York*, where I arrived that Night. In the Morning I waited upon the
Governor, and presented to him my Credentials from my first Master,
as to my Business. He order'd me to continue at his House till further
Notice, and the Servants helped me to what I stood in need of.

Colonel *Crosby* the Governor,[19] was an *Irishman*, and formerly a common Soldier; but being a graceful Man, had the Address to gain the
Affection of Lord *Halifax's* Sister, and married her, which raised him to
the Posts he enjoys. He had two Daughters, both handsome Ladies. The
Eldest was married to the Lord *Augustus Fitzroy*, Second Son to the Duke
of *Grafton*. The youngest is unmarried. This Marriage was just then

19. William Cosby (ca. 1695–1736) served as governor of New York from 1731 to 1736.

discovered, which gave a great deal of Uneasiness to the Family, because the Father was a Stranger to it; but the Matter was soon made up by the Lord *Baltimore* with the Duke of *Grafton*.

The next Day the Governor order'd me two Clocks to clean, for which he gave me two Pistoles,[20] and recommended me to several Gentlemen of Figure, from whom I got Money. But my Creditors joining together, made one Debt of it, and followed me to *New York*, by a Letter to an Attorney; which I having Notice of, immediately apply'd to Capt. *Ingoldsby*, Commander of the Fort, and Son to the Late Lieutenant General *Ingoldsby*, Commander of her late Majesty Queen *Anne's* Troops in *Ireland*, who admitted me as a Soldier: So that the Attorney applying to the Captain, had no Remedy.

Escaping this Snare, I continued at *New York*, and liv'd as a Servant with a *Spanish* Gentleman, named *Don Roderigo de Almeria*, of *Valentia*. I liv'd a very sober, retir'd Life, and obtain'd this Gentleman's Favour, by my Assiduity in serving him. He made me his Confident, and related to me his Adventures, which are, in his own Words, as follows.

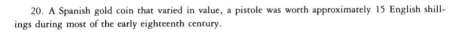

20. A Spanish gold coin that varied in value, a pistole was worth approximately 15 English shillings during most of the early eighteenth century.

AT *Valentia*, chief City of the Kingdom of that Name, the richest, pleasant, and most fertile Kingdom in *Spain*, liv'd *Don Roderigo de Almeria*, descended from the Dukes of *Medina Coeli*, First Peers of *Spain*. He enjoy'd a plentiful Estate, besides an honourable Post he held under the King, being Comptroller of the Finances of *Valentia*. He married *Donna Jacinta*, Daughter of *Don Pedro Torruga*, a Gentleman of Fortune at *Malaga*. By her he had three Sons, myself being the youngest, and named after him. My eldest Brother, *Don Sancho*, was sent into the Wars against the Emperor.

I continued at home with my Father, being design'd for a religious Habit; but that Life not suiting with my Inclination, I expostulated with my Father, and told him, I was inclin'd to follow the Law, notwithstanding an Education was given me to qualify me for the former Profession. My Father giving Ear to my Request, sent me to *Malaga*, where I studied the Law under the Direction of *Don Manuel Lopes de Gusman*, and acquir'd, by my Assiduity, a general Applause.

There lived in the Neighbourhood, a Lady, Daughter of a considerable Banker, nam'd, *Sebastian de la Vega*. She was young and beautiful, and possess'd of all the good Qualities which seldom fail of making a complete Woman. I conceiv'd a Passion for her, infinitely beyond Expression. My first Sight of her was at a *Villa*, some small Distance from *Malaga*; and at my Return, I made it my chief Business to find out the Mistress of my Affections, which I soon effected by means of an old *Duena* who was kept in the Family.

At this Time I made a Figure suitable to the Grandeur of my Family, having large Remittances from my Father. This *Duena* passing by near the House where I liv'd, I gave her a Letter, with some Money, promising, if she acquitted herself faithfully, I'd make her a handsome Recompence. She promis'd me she would, and parted. I follow'd her to the House, and perceiv'd she deliver'd my Letter to the Object of my Wishes. I waited some Days, expecting her Answer; when a Servant brought me a Billet, and left me abruptly. I hastily open'd it, and read the following Words.

To Don Roderigo de Almeria.

SIR,

I Am very much surpris'd to find a Gentleman should express a Passion for a Lady with whom he has not the least Acquaintance. For me, I am under the Direction of a Father, to whom I owe all possible Love and Obedience; and can never grant a Heart to any other, without his Approbation. You are at your own Disposal, and unless you apply in a proper Manner, can receive no Admittance from

JAQUELINA.

This answer'd my Expectation, and I was as much charm'd with her Prudence as her Person; but not knowing which Way to apply to her Father, ten thousand Thoughts revolv'd in my Mind. But he having, soon after, a Contest at Law, my good Fortune brought me acquainted with him; for by the Recommendation of a neighbouring Gentleman, I became his Advocate, had an Opportunity of visiting him, and by him was introduc'd to the Acquaintance of the incomparable *Donna Jaquelina*. The Law-suit was ended to his Advantage, and I received the Applause of the Court, and the Thanks of the Family.

This made *Don Sebastian* enquire after my Family, and being informed to his Satisfaction, told *Donna Jaquelina*, she must not look upon me as a Person necessitated to follow the Law, but as one descended of the first House in *Spain*; which coming to my hearing, by the Means of the old *Duena*, I received at all Times, an easy Admittance, which imbolden'd me to declare my Passion to her the first favourable Opportunity that should offer.

The next Day as I was passing by the Church, called *Notre Dame de Dios*, I perceived a Lady advancing towards me, and discovered her to be the charming *Jaquelina*; and putting a Face upon it, I addressed her in the most civil Manner. Madam, says I, you are sensible of the entire Affection I have for you, and hope you will give me leave to return you my Thanks for the many Happinesses I enjoy in your Conversation. I was going on when she stopped me, by turning short, and stepping into the Church.

This affected me to such a Degree, that I became Thunderstruck, but composing myself, I stay'd till she return'd; and then accosting her with the greatest Respect, begged her Pardon for my Rudeness, and declared to her, in the sincerest Manner, that from the first Time I ever saw her, I became her Slave, and that no Consideration could prevail with me to withdraw my Affection.

A Declaration of this Nature surprized the lovely *Jaquelina*, but recovering herself from her Confusion, and, blushing, said, Sir, I am subject to the Obedience of a tender Father, and without his Consent can never part with a Heart intirely at his Disposal. I then told her I was the Person to whom she directed a Billet, and protested that I wou'd sacrifice to her all other Considerations. We parted, and I returned home.

A few Days after *Don Sebastian* invited me to his House, when I received a Proof of his good Intentions. He declared to me, that as he had an only Daughter, he had some Inclination to dispose of her, and if I would accept of the Proposal, he should think himself honoured by such an Alliance. I humbly thanked him for his Offer, and told him, I intended to have asked the Favour of him, but was glad to find he had such a good Opinion of me, and accepted his Offer. After which I told her what had passed, and she with some reluctancy yielded to my Wishes, and a Day was appointed for the Solemnization of the Nuptials.

Before this an unlucky Accident happen'd, that made me the most miserable of Mankind. The Arrival of my second Brother, *Don Frederick*, who, with a magnificent Equipage, attracted the Eyes of the Citizens of *Malaga*. He took up his Residence at the Palace of the *Count de Mon-*

temar, the Governor, where I repaired to congratulate him on his safe Arrival. He received me with an Affection suitable to the Relation between us; when I told him of my intended Marriage, and invited him to grace my Nuptials with his Presence.

Some Days after I took him along with me, and introduced him into the House of *Don Sebestian*; where, on my Account, he met with a noble Reception. But after some few Days, I perceived I was received at the House with Coldness, and soon after was denyed Admittance, being told my Brother was more welcome. I upbraided him with his Breach of Friendship; but he denyed he had any Design to supplant me.

Soon after he married *Jaquelina*, which when I heard, I resolved to leave *Malaga*. To which Intent, I sold off all my Moveables, and, unknown either to my Brother or Acquaintance, left the Place, and went to my Father at *Valentia*, whom I made acquainted with my Brother's deceitful Dealings. He pacified me in the most moving Terms, and said, He would advance my Fortune, advising me to go to *Naples*.

Shortly after I sail'd with a Cargo of about Eight Thousand Pieces of Eight; but was taken by an *Algerine* Pirate, and carried to *Algiers*, where I continued a Slave three Years, and underwent inexpressible Hardships. But my Father hearing of my Disaster, soon redeemed me for 500 Pistoles, and I returned to *Valentia*.

I went afterwards with a Cargo to *Florida*; but that Place being unhealthy, I went to the *English* Colonies, and settled at *New York*, where I heard of the Death of my Second Brother. I then resolved to leave *America*, and sail'd in a *Dutch* Vessel bound to *Spain*. After a tedious Voyage, we arrived at *Gibraltar* where my Father gave me a welcome Reception, and desired me not to think of parting from him. Soon after News was brought us of the Death of my Elder Brother; so I became universal Heir to my Father's Estate.

The former Disappointment I met with as to *Jaquelina*, had not cured me, for now I was resolved to renew my Suit; to which Intent I stole from my Father, under Pretence of a Visit to *Don Hieronimo Gonzalez*, President of *Malaga*; and being attended by a Valet, set forward, and arrived there, where I inquired after her.

One Day as I was walking near the Arsenal, I perceived her in a Widow's Dress, and making an Obeisance, cryed, Dear *Jaquelina!* It is impossible to conceive the Confusion she was in at the Sight of me. She fixed her Eyes on me, and said, *Don Roderigo!* I recovered myself from my first surprize, and desired her to relate to me her Father's Unkindness. She protested to me, that from the first Time I addressed her, she conceived an Esteem for me, and what she did, was by compulsion of her Father; and since my Departure, she was under the greatest Concern for my Welfare.

Then she desired me to stay with her, telling me, That since the Death of my Brother, she had resolved to give her Heart to no other Person but my self; and that all she had was at my Disposal. I caused Articles of Marriage to be drawn, but an Objection was made as to the Validity of my Marriage; when I applied to the Archbishop of *Toledo* for a Dispensation, who procured me a Bull from *Rome*, invalidating my Brother's Marriage, upon the Account of a Pre-contract between myself and *Donna Jaquelina*.

I lived many Years with her, but Death parted us, which so sensible afflicted me, that I resolved to leave the World, and retire to a Monastry. Before this my Father died, when I sold my Estate, and gave the greatest Part to the Poor. Here I resigned myself to the Will of God, renouncing the Vanities of this troublesome World; but happening to find a Book wrote by the Archbishop of *Canterbury*, Dr. *Tillotson*, which levelled at the *Romish* Superstition, I became a Convert, and resolved to escape.[1] So with some Difficulty I transported myself to *London*, where I publickly renounced the Errors of the Church of *Rome*.

From *London* I embarked for *New York*, where I advanced my Fortune by Trade; but having an Inclination to spend the Remainder of my Day at *London*, in order to be thoroughly initiated into the Principles of the *Reformed Religion*, I now wait for a Ship to transport me thither for that Intent.

---

1. Dr. John Tillotson (1630–94) was Archbishop of Canterbury and author of a polemic against Roman Catholicism, "The Rule of Faith" (1666).

10   DEPARTURE FROM NEW YORK—DUCKING
WITCHES AT MOUNT HOLLY—LOADING
SHIP—JOURNEY TO MARYLAND—ENCOUNTER WITH
A HORN SNAKE—ASSISTS A MOTHER AND TWO
CHILDREN—DANGER FROM CREDITORS—SETS SAIL
FOR IRELAND—THE MAN WITH THREE WIVES.

AFTER I had continued with this Gentleman some time, I returned towards *Burlington*, and went and lived with my first Master, who sent me to *Mount Holly*, where I was witness to one of the strangest Pieces of Folly that was ever acted. Certain old Women, of Melancholick Physognomy,[1] had got the Character of Witches; and being questioned on that Account, and not able to clear themselves, were obliged to undergo a Ducking, in order to prove whether or no they were such.

The Notion run, if they sunk, they were no Witches; but if they swam, they were, and shou'd be punished as such. But they miraculously escaped the Censure of the Law, by sinking, tho' they remained a considerable Time on the Surface of the Water. But this not satisfying one *Jonathan Wright*,[2] he proposed to weigh them in Scales against the

1. A kind of madness evidenced in facial features.
2. On Jonathan Wright, see Appendix H.

Bible, and concluded, if they were Witches, they would not weigh so heavy as the Bible; but to the Surprise of the Beholders, they weighed down both Prophets and Apostles.[3]

After this foolish Adventure, I went back to *Burlington*, and lived again with the Blacksmith. This being the Time they gather the *Indian* Corn into their Grannaries, the Townspeople were busy in husking it for that Purpose. The Neighbours assist one another in stripping the Corn from the Husks, and are treated with Rum and Punch; but Persons of Figure provide a grand Entertainment. Every Night, for a Fortnight, I was busy at one or other of these Meetings.

I now began to be heartily tir'd with these Ramblings, and endeavoured to make Friends with Masters of Ships, in order to get my Passage. One Morning, as I was forging a Horse Shoe, a grave Quaker, one *Thomas Wetheril*, of *Workington*, in *Cumberland*, told me, He found the Business I follow'd would do little for me, and advis'd me to return Home, where he heard I had considerable Relations. He said he had recommended me to Capt. *Peel*, whose Ship then lay at the Key, and would sail in about five Weeks.

I who had before resolv'd to embrace the first Opportunity that offer'd readily entered into his Measures, immediately left the Horse Shoe unfinished, and went to the Ship, where the Captain was, and told him Mr *Wetheril* had sent me. He ask'd me if I was a Sailor; if not, if I would undertake to be Cook on board, he would give me my Passage, and on our arrival at *Ireland*, assist me with Money, to enable me to go to *Newcastle*. I immediately struck a Bargain, and at his Desire assisted the Crew in stowing the Ship with Logs, Hogsheads, and Pipe Staves,[4] he giving me Liberty to leave the Ship when any Business in my Way offer'd.

But the most difficult Task I had to undertake was splitting of Wood for Firing. This Wood was four Feet in Length; and the Materials for splitting, were an Ax and a Wedge. I was so awkward in my first Essay, that I feared I should not be able to compleat my Task, and consequently lose my Passage; which the Master perceiving, laugh'd, and generously gave me such Directions as enabled me to acquit Myself manfully, which I did in three Days, to his and my own Satisfaction.

---

3. A story about this event also appeared in the *Pennsylvania Gazette*, October 15–22, 1730. A more complete discussion of the episode and the reprinted newspaper article are available in Appendix H.

4. Hogsheads were large casks, and pipe staves were boards used for making pipes to hold liquids, primarily wine.

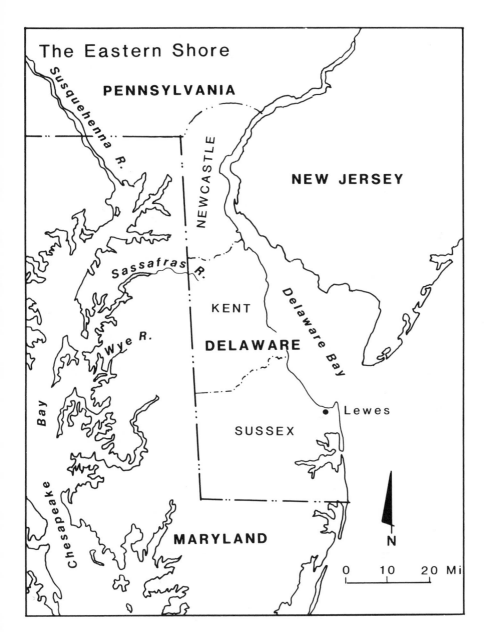

Map 4. The Eastern Shore.

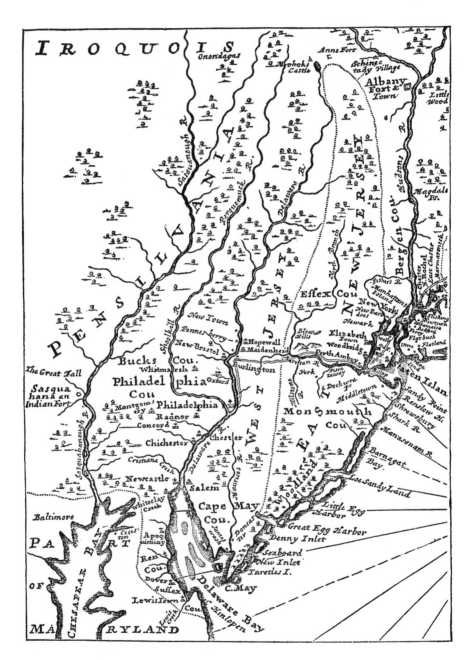

Map 5. The Province of Pennsylvania, 1730. This depiction, like many other maps drawn during this era, is somewhat inaccurate, which may account in part for Moraley's difficulty in finding his way through the countryside.

I afterwards carried Pipe Staves on my Shoulders, from the Land to the Ship, to the number of above thirty-six thousand. In a Fortnight after our Ship was loaded, when we had nothing else to do but to eat and drink, the Captain allowing us hot Meat Morning, Noon, and Night. But having about three Weeks on my Hands, I resolv'd to take a small Journey towards *Maryland*, and pass'd through the Counties of *Newcastle, Kent,* and *Sussex.* These are subject to the Province of *Pensilvania,* and are very unhealthy, being swampy Ground, and Fevers raging continually.

Newcastle is chief of the three Counties, the Assembly being kept there. *Lewes,* near the Sea, in *Sussex,* is a Fishing Town. I pass'd by *Bohemia Head* into *Maryland,* after I had crossed the Rivers *Susquehannah* and *Sassafras,* so call'd from abundance of those Trees growing along its Banks. Then *Wye* River, near which lived a Roman Catholick Gentleman, named *Richard Bennet,*[5] commonly call'd, *Poor Dick of Wye,* though the richest Man in those Parts. I soon after pass'd *Potomack* River, and went to Col. *Mason,*[6] a near Relation of my Mother's and was well receiv'd.[7] He invited me to stay; but fearing I should lose my Passage, I return'd back, he giving me six Pieces of Eight to bear my Expenses.

In a Wood near a Place call'd *Oppoquinomy,* I espied a Snake lying in a Path-way; and endeavouring to shun it by going out of the Road, I accidentally trod upon another, which immediately twisted itself about my Right Leg, and squeez'd it so hard, that I was afraid it would have broke. After I had stood some time, expecting to be bit, the Snake dropp'd upon the Ground, and I came off unhurt. I viewed it, and

5. Richard Bennet died in 1749 at age eighty-three at his seat in Queen Ann County. The local newspaper reported that he was "supposed to be the richest man in America." See Robert Barnes, *Marriages and Deaths from the Maryland Gazette, 1727–1839* (Baltimore: Genealogical Publishing Co., 1973), 11.

6. The primary residence of Colonel George Mason (1690–1735) was at Chickamuxon Creek, Charles County, Maryland, but Mason owned another estate across the Potomac River in Virginia. Because he was the third generation of Masons to live on the Chesapeake Bay, it is not clear how Moraley's mother, Martha Mason, could have been closely related, although it would not have been impossible. See Pamela C. Copeland and Richard K. MacMaster, *The Five George Masons: Patriots and Planters of Virginia and Maryland* (Charlottesville: University Press of Virginia, 1975), 56 and genealogical appendixes.

7. Moraley does not remember his route correctly. First, Lewes is far to the south, at the mouth of the Delaware Bay. Second, because the Susquehanna River drains into the northwest part of the Chesapeake Bay and the Sassafras and Wye rivers are on the eastern shore of the bay, Moraley could not have crossed all three in his journey south. Finally, the Potomac River separates Maryland and Virginia, so Moraley would have entered the latter colony if he crossed that river. Moraley may have visited Mason on the eastern shore of Maryland. Map 4 provides the correct geographic features of the eastern shore, while Map 5 shows a common but incorrect geographical understanding of the area in 1730.

found I had tread upon the Head, which prevented its Biting. I look'd upon this as a Mercy, and return'd Thanks to the Author of Good for my Deliverance. It was a Horn Snake, six Foot long.

The next Day I met a Woman, with two Children, walking the same Road. She had miss'd her Way, and desir'd me to direct her. I found she was bound to *Philadelphia*, and proffer'd to be assistant to her, upon Occasion, to carry her youngest Child, which was not three Years old, the other being about nine; and she in return bore my Charges. The second Day after we travell'd together, Night coming on, we were ob-lig'd to take our Lodging all Night under an Oak Tree, where you may depend I was not uncivil to her. It was in the Month of *August*; and the Weather being excessive warm, we were constrain'd to keep awake for fear of the Bears, which often roam about in the Night. In the Morning we proceeded towards *Bohemia Head*, and in two Days reach'd *Philadelphia*, where we parted.

From thence I went to *Burlington*, and repair'd to the Ship, when we had Notice to prepare for sailing in three Days. The Day being come, the Captain invited all his Friends on board, to take his Farewel of them; and I was order'd to clean my Kettles and Plates, and boil a Quarter of Mutton, and some Beef. The Company consisted of about 40 Persons. I serv'd up Dinner, receiv'd the Thanks of all present for my good Management, and the Punch Bowl going merrily about, I made a shift to get myself drunk before Three o'Clock. Whilst we were carous-ing, who should come to the Ship but the Woman I was speaking of before, and agreed with the Captain for her and her Children's Passage.

We stay'd four or five Days at *Philadelphia*, in order to take in more Provisions, during which Time I was frequently sent on Shore to fetch and carry Bottles for the Use of the Captain, when I was discovered by my Creditors, which put me into a Pannick Fear; but acquainting the Captain, he secured me close on board, where I guarded the Ship by myself, the Sailors being always on Shore taking their Leave of their Mistresses and Friends.

One Day as I was walking the Deck, a Boat came along Side of us, having a Gentleman in her, who desired Admittance. He was a hand-some young *Irishman*, a Surgeon by Profession, but very much in Debt. I secured him in the Cabbin, but the next Morning he venturing upon Deck, the Water Bailiff[8] enter'd, seized and carried him to Jail for one Hundred and Forty Pounds.

8. The port authorities.

On the 26th of July, we sailed down [the] *Delaware*, and the next Day passed by *Chester*, Capital of the County of the same Name.[9] It is seated close to the River, and contains about two hundred Houses, adorn'd with pleasant Gardens and Orchards. There I was overtaken by my old Master *Edmund Lewis*, who demanded me of the Captain, on account of an Indenture between myself and him, but the Boat being in Haste, oblig'd him to step into her, otherwise he must have gone to Sea with us, the Ship being under Sail and so I escaped being carried back.

From hence we arrived at *Newcastle*, where we cast Anchor, and sent a Boat on Shore to buy more fresh Provisions. I was one and going to a House some Distance from the Town, we bought a Quarter of Mutton, and a Quarter of Beef. Myself and the Crew went into a Back Yard, where, with the help of a Stick and a Stone, we knocked down five Geese, and brought them on board, tying them by the Necks round our Waists, like *Aesop's* Goslings, to prevent their Cackling. After this Exploit we returned on board. *Newcastle* is a large Town, of about 400 Houses, neatly built, and inhabited by wealthy People.

The next Day, in the Morning, we perceived a lame Wild Goose swimming on the Surface of the Water, and a Bald Eagle attempting several times to seize her, which we prevented by shooting him, and sent a Boat, which took the Goose, of which we made a Sea Pye.

In the Afternoon a Boat came along the Ship's Side, and demanded to speak with the Captain, who came up, and they complained to him of the Loss of their Geese, and demanded Satisfaction. All Hands were called upon Deck, and the Captain asked every one of us, if we knew any thing concerning the Geese. We all stiffly denyed we had, or knew any thing about, them. So the Boat left us.

About Two in the Afternoon on the next Day, the Captain being upon Deck, with myself, the Geese being hungry, cackled. The Master hearing them, said to me, *How cou'd you have the Impudence to deny them*, and call'd up the Crew, and upbraided them with their Theft: But a brisk young Fellow boldly told him, that considering we had a long Voyage before us, and our Provisions but scanty, we thought we were obliged to take what lay in our Way, and wou'd pay for the Geese when we returned. The Captain laugh'd, and order'd me to kill one of them for Dinner. So I open'd the Forecastle, where I had stored my Firewood

9. The *Sea Flower*, commanded by Captain Oswald Peel, actually left Philadelphia during the week of September 19–26, 1734, according to the *Pennsylvania Gazette* published that week. The ship's destination was Dublin, Ireland. It had arrived in Philadelphia from Barbados on July 4.

and the Geese, and executed the Captain's Command, and roasted one of them for Dinner.

The next Day, the Wind proving favourable, we sailed down the River for the Capes, in two Days passed them, and in Two more sail'd above four hundred Miles; but the Wind shifting, we were obliged to lye by; a brisk Gale suddenly arising, we steer'd our Course towards *Ireland*; but an unlucky Mischance happen'd, for the Ship sprung a Leak, which obliged us to pump continually, changing Hands every half Hour, which harassed us to such a Degree, that if it had not been for God's Providence, we must have sunk under the Fatigue; but the Leak stopp'd by Pumping, and the Dirt on the Sides of the Ship getting into the Gap, we escaped. It was impossible to unload to find out the Defect, because we were full of Wood, wedg'd very close and hard.

We had in our Company the *Irish* Woman, a *Scotchman*, and an *Irishman*, named *Mullen*, who had three Wives, one at *Dublin*, one at *Philadelphia*, and one at *London*. Our Employment, during our Voyage, was diverting our selves with relating our Adventures; at other Times we washed our Linen. For my Part, I had but one Shirt to my back, and consequently had little Care on that account; so my chief Business was to endeavour to please the Company with my Cookery.

journey to newcastle

11   VOYAGE TO IRELAND—DUBLIN HARBOUR—
ARRIVES AT WORKINGTON—"THE PICTURE OF
ROBINSON CRUSOE"—"A GRAVE QUAKER"—MERRY
MAKING—NETHER HALL—A TANKARD OF
SUPERNACULUM—MR. SENHOUSE'S
PLEASANTRIES—CROSBY.

T HE Wind was not generally favourable to us, and we were eleven Weeks before we had any hopes of a Sight of the desir'd Port. But about 300 Miles, by the Computation of our Sailing, we discover'd a Ship, and made up to her. She prov'd a *Dublin* Ship from *Portugal*. The Captain agreed with us in our Reckning; but we out-sailing him, lost sight of them in the Night.

The next Day, I being under Deck, the Captain call'd me up to see a monstrous Whale, about two Miles from us, frisking upon the Waters, then diving down head foremost, and spouting Water from him. Afterwards we saw several large Birds, call'd *Gannets*, but by the *Scots* and *Irish, Solen Geese*; from which our Captain conjectur'd we were not far from Land. This prov'd true, for the next Day we got into Soundings, which we discover'd by our Plummets;[1] and in two Hours after saw the Western Coast of *Ireland*, near Cape *Clear*. We steer'd round the South-

1. The sailors discovered the sea bottom by dropping a piece of metal attached to a line.

ern Coast, and after we pass'd *Cork* and *Kingsale*, arriv'd in the Harbour
of *Dublin*, after above thirteen Weeks Sail, and cast Anchor near *Rings-
end*, not far from *Aston's Key*, from whence we discover'd the two Cathe-
drals, and had a Prospect of that famous City.

Here our Passengers left us; and the *Irishman* who had three Wives,
skulk'd about Town for fear of his Wife. The *Irish* Woman I met in
America, left us to go to her Father, who refus'd her Admittance to his
House, bidding her go to her Husband in *Carolina*. For you must know,
that about nine Years before her Arrival at *Dublin*, she had married an
old Man, (by her Father's Orders, but entirely against her own Inclination) whose Effects lying at *Charles Town*, in *South Carolina*, they were
forced to go thither; when she, repenting her Match, elop'd from him,
and robb'd him of all his Household Furniture, which she sent by Sea to
Philadelphia, herself and Children travelling it by Land on Foot.[2]

The Captain one Day coming on board, for he and the Men went
every Day ashore, leaving me to stay by the Ship, I desir'd to be dismiss'd; but he told me, that as soon as he had sold the Cargo, he would
carry me to *Whitehaven*, where he had a Mother and two Sisters living.
But shortly after this, not disposing of his Goods, he was for sailing to
Carlingford, about 36 Miles from *Dublin*, which disappointed me for the
present.

About a Week after, there being a Collier[3] bound to *Workington*, in
Cumberland, which was to sail the next Morning, I desired the Mate to
dismiss me; to which he agreed, and sent four Hands with me in the
Boat to the Ship, nam'd the *Leviathan*, Captain *Steel*, where I had a
hearty Welcome from the generous Commander.

I observed the two Nights I was with him both Morning and Evening he read Prayers to the Crew. It was the only Ship I was ever in
where there was no Swearing or prophane Talking. We set Sail at Seven

2. The mysterious Irish woman who robbed her husband and left him in Charles Town (Charleston) to return to Dublin could have been Mary Townsend. The following advertisement appeared in
the Charleston newspaper on March 16, 1734: "Whereas a chaise, several parcels of linen, household
goods, plate, and other things were lately stolen from my Plantation near the Quarter House and
supposed to be concealed by some evil persons in and about Charlestown. A reward is offered for their
discovery. All persons are cautioned against buying my cattle or other things from Mary Townsend, my
now wife, as I will not allow receipt to be given by her and am not responsible for her debts.—J.
Townsend." Other notices indicate that Joseph Townsend was involved in many local quarrels. See
Alton T. Moran, *The South Carolina Gazette: Genealogical Abstracts, 1732–1735* (Bowie, Md.: Heritage
Books, 1987), 64–65.

3. A coal-carrying vessel.

in the Morning with a constant fair Wind, and after seven Hours sailing, we passed by the *Isle of Man*, and reached *Workington*. The next Day, about eight in the Morning, a Custom Officer, named *Lowther*, boarded us, and, pitying my Condition, gave me a Note directed to Mr *Senhouse* of *Nether Hall*.[4] I got two Drams[5] before my Departure, took my Leave of the Ship, and set my foot upon *English* Ground, after three Years and eight Months Absence.

 - I was drest in the following Trim. I had a Shirt on above fourteen or fifteen Weeks, a miserable Pair of Breeches, adorn'd with many living Companions, two torn Waistcoats, no Coat, a coarse, lousy, Woolen Cap, an old Hat given me in *Ireland*, a Pair of torn Stockings, a bad Pair of Shoes supported by Packthread,[6] no Handkerchief: So I looked not unlike the Picture of *Robinson Crusoe*.

With these Disadvantages I was to travel about fourscore Miles before I reach'd *Newcastle*, through a Country where I was not known, and at the worst Time of the Year, it being the Day after *Christmas Day*, and so rainy, that for the nine Days I was trampousing home, there was scarce any Intermission, which very much discourag'd me; but making a Virtue of Necessity, I comforted myself with the Prospect of getting home, where I did not doubt of having the Fatted Calf kill'd for me.

I enter'd the Town of *Workington*, at that time very dirty, which being a Specimen of the Terribleness of the remaining Part of my Journey, I was uneasy, for I had not one Farthing[7] about me. So walking about the Town, musing on Ways and Means how I should get Intelligence of the right Road, a grave Quaker, sitting at his Door, ask'd me where I was bound. I readily acquiesc'd with his Demand, and he gave me Two-pence,[8] the first Money I had finger'd since I left *America*.

So leaving him, I repair'd to *Workington Hall*, the Seat of the *Curwens*; but not meeting with Encouragement, I remember'd Mr *Lowther's* Note to Mr *Senhouse*, and endeavour'd to inform myself of his Abode. So leaving this dirty Town, I met with two Gentleman's Servants, who told me they were going a merry making, and said if I would accompany them, they would direct me in the Road to *Nether Hall*. I readily

---

4. Humphrey Senhouse of Netherhall, Cumberland, is mentioned briefly in Stephen and Lee, *Dictionary of National Biography*, 17:1182.

5. A "dram" is a small draught of alcohol.

6. A stout thread or twine often used for tying bundles.

7. One-fourth of a pence.

8. Twelve pence equaled one shilling.

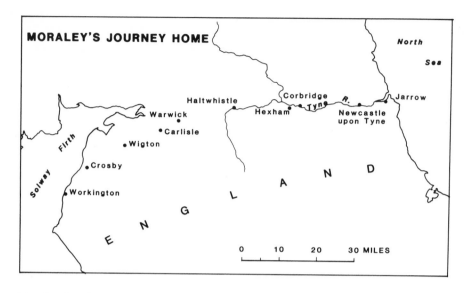

Map 6.   Moraley's journey home.

chew? funny way to say it.

agreed to follow them, hoping by their means I should have an Opportunity to exercise my Grinders, being hungry; and my Desire was ac-
complish'd, for we had not travell'd long before an Alehouse presented
itself to our View, when I gladly heard them propose to bait.[9] So we
enter'd the House, where we drank two Quarts of Ale, and I being
sharp set, desir'd something to eat. Accordingly a Plate of Goose Pye
was brought, which I soon dispatch'd.

The Reckning being paid, we proceeded forward, when one of the
Persons looking steadfastly at me, said he knew me, and then told me
he was one of those who carried my Mother and Mr *Brown* in a Boat to
Jarrow, to be married.[10] This I was a Stranger to, as to Mr *Brown's*
Marriage with her; tho' I knew at *Philadelphia* she was married to a

9. To eat.

10. Moraley's mother, Martha Isaacson, wed for the third time to Thomas Brown on September 25,
1732, at South Shields, a town east of Jarrow and also on the south side of the Tyne River (IGI). The
marriage bond taken out on August 9, 1732, lists Thomas Brown of Newcastle as an armiger—that is,
a man entitled to armorial bearings, a gentleman or squire; his co-signer on the bond, Matthew Daw-
son, was also a gentleman (*Durham Marriage Bonds, 1730–1738* [Microfilm, Family History Library,
Salt Lake City, British Film Area #1040263], 63). The former Martha Mason, who had inherited some
valuable property from her first husband, seems to have consistently improved her social standing
through marriage, advancing from wife of a watchmaker to wife of a Captain and then of a gentleman.

Justice of the Peace, which in some measure occasion'd me to come home.

Parting from these two Men, I travell'd I know not where, to find out *Nether Hall*; but not meeting with any body to give me Information, I rambled till it began to grow Dark; when, as good Luck would have it, I discovered a new House, which I made up to, and perceiving a good-look'd Man, he invited me in, gave me two Pints of good Ale, and directed me to *Nether Hall*. So steering from thence, after much Difficulty, through Dirt and Water, I discover'd an old Castle at a good Distance, and made up to it; but several Water Places intervening, I was obliged to wade through them, up to the Waist, before I could get to the Castle, when I discovered a Light.

After passing a small Bridge, before a Garden adorn'd with Leaden Images, I enter'd the Kitchen, wherein were an old Lady turning a Beef Stake with a Pair of Beef Tongs, attended by the Household Steward and his Wife, a good pretty Woman, and House-keeper to the Family. Upon my first approach, I asked for Mr *Senhouse*, and, stepping forward, the Lady asked me from whence I came, and where bound; which having answered to effect, she demanded what Trade I followed: To which I answer'd, Clock and Watch-making was my Business. Says she, You look more like a Chimney Sweeper. Madam, answer'd I, it is no Wonder, I should make such an Appearance, considering the Hardships I have undergone in my Voyage.

She was going on when Mr *Senhouse* came down Stairs into the Kitchen, and demanded my Business; so producing my Credentials from Mr *Lowther*, he bad me sit down. Then surveying my external Edifice, he asked where I intended to lye that Night. I answer'd, Where God's good Providence directed me. Well, said he, for that Expression you shall not be exposed to the Inclemency of the Weather: I will provide for you To-night, and To-morrow will give you such Security, as will carry you home.

Then he ask'd me, if I knew any Body at *Newcastle*. To which I answer'd, I knew almost every Body. He said, Do you know the Recorder?[11] Yes, Sir, said I, I have Reason to know him. Why, who is he? What is his Name, says he? To which I replyed, His Name is *Isaacson*; his Brother, Capt. *Charles Isaacson*, married my Mother. Thus making myself known, had a good Effect; for he, in the first Place, order'd a brown Toast, and a Tankard of *Supernaculum*, to be given me. Then

11. Magistrate or judge.

order'd his Steward to get me some Necessaries. The Steward brought me an old Coat, about half a Yard too long for me, an old Wig, an old Pair of Hose, and a good Shirt worth about Ten Shillings. The Footman was ordered to shave me, which he did, and bereaved me of a troublesome Companion in so doing, for he had been my Chum for above 14 Weeks.

Mr *Senhouse* coming in soon after I was renovated, asked me pleasantly which of his Maids I liked best. To which I replyed, They were so agreeable, that I could not prefer the one to the other. After some merry Discourse had pass'd, I went to Bed, and sleep'd for the first Time in a Bed since I had left *Philadelphia*. In the Morning the Servant awaked me, and said his Master desired me to come to him. He was in the Kitchen waiting for me, when he gave me four Half Crowns,[12] and a recommendatory Letter to divers Gentlemen on the Road. And told me, He expected me to write to him when I got home, otherwise he should not think I was the same Person I said I was.

After promising him that I would write to him when I arrived at *Newcastle*, I proceeded towards a little Town near the Sea, called *Crosby*. At my first Enterance, I perceived a Parson smoking a Pipe; by his Appearance he seemed the Curate.[13] He accosted me in a civil Manner, and invited me to his House, which was a neat Place, indifferently furnished; the best of his Goods being a handsome brown Wife, dress'd in a clean brown Gown, and a blue Topknot. Here I drank two Pints of his good Ale, and smoaked a Pipe. It is a hundred to one if the Vicar[14] would have regaled me so well; for Men in plentiful Circumstances, seldom or never consider the Wants of the Needy.

He directed me to one *Harriman*, a Clock-maker, living at the Upper-end of the Town, who was very civil to me, and invited me to stay with him two or three Days, till I had recovered the Fatigues of my Voyage, which I did, and assisted him in two or three Jobs in my Way, and departed from him towards *Tallontire Hall*, the Seat of Mr *Partis*, where I arrived about Eleven in the Morning, and enter'd the Kitchen, where Mrs *Partis* was making White Puddings.[15] Upon my making myself known, she caused to be brought in a Quart of as good Beer as ever I drank in my Life, and I eat the best Part of the Ribs of a Quarter of Lamb.

---

12. A half crown was the equivalent of 2 shillings and 6 pence.
13. A clergyman who acts in the capacity of a deputy or assistant.
14. A parish priest who receives a stipend.
15. Part of the stomach or entrails of an animal stuffed with a mixture of minced meat, oatmeal, seasoning, and other assorted items.

STILL SEARCHING FOR STEADY EMPLOYMENT

THEN leaving her, I marched towards *Hayton Castle*, the Seat of
the late Sir *Richard Musgrave*, Bar[one]t and on *Saturday* in the Evening
reached the Town; when hearing the Tooting of a Bag-pipe, I fancied it
was an Ale-house, and was not deceived in my Conjecture. The first
Thing I said here was, If I could have a Lodging. The Landlady said,
Have you any Money? Yes, said I, and put a half Crown between my
Teeth. Sir, says the old Bedlam,[1] you are welcome; will you have any
Thing to eat. To which I answer'd, With all my Heart. She set before
me a Plate charged with Goose Pye; the Intelects were good enough,
but the external Frame was as brown as the Parson's Wife's Face, spoken
of before.

After I had finished my Meal, a Man in the Chimney Corner called
me by Name, and desired me to do as he did: There were three Men

---

1. "Bedlam" is a term for a person suited for a lunatic asylum, although Moraley may have meant
"beldam," a common eighteenth-century pejorative term meaning an old woman.

with him, they drank Brandy and Ale, to the Tune of four Quarts, which made me so merry, that I danced with the Piper.[2] Afterwards the Company paid their Reckoning and departed, and I went to Bed. The next Morning I drank a Quart of Ale, paid for it, and proceeded to the Castle of Sir *Richard Musgrave*. In the Kitchen were Three or Four of his Servants, who I begg'd to tell their Master I desired to speak with him. He appeared, and ordered me a Horn of Drink,[3] which was given me, with Three Shillings.

Then I pass'd through a Road between *Hayton* and *Sparetree*, and baited at the Sign of the *Blue Anchor*, which was occupied by a handsome young Landlady, who gave me some Goose Pye, and two Pots of Ale. From thence, about Eleven, I arriv'd at *Sparetree*, a pitiful dirty Hole, having a Church. Passing thro', I perceiv'd a Coach with a Gentleman in it, which was our Collector *Lawson's* Son, preceded by the Family Steward,[4] who with a surly Tone ask'd me where I was bound. But I not regarding him nor his Demand, went directly to *Brighton Hall*, the Seat of *Gilfred Lawson*, Esq; who was walking in his Kitchen Garden, in a *Scotch* Plad Night Gown. He very civily ask'd me where I was going; which having resolv'd, he order'd me two Horns of Ale, and a new Three Half-penny Brick,[5] with some Potted Beef, and gave me two Shillings. Afterwards he gave me another Shilling, and directed me to *Wigton*, about seven Miles from his House.

Here, after four Hours Travel, over Hills and Dales, thro' Rain and Dirt, I discover'd the Church when almost dark and enter'd the Town, a small Place, and every other House in it an Ale-house; so, consequently, they have no Trade but on the Market days. I quarter'd at the *George*; but having considered I had a long Journey home, I got up the next Morning by Four o'Clock, taking my Route to *Carlisle*, which I reach'd at Three that Afternoon, and took up my Residence at the *Royal Oak*. Here I got acquainted with a Watch-maker, and did a Job, for which I got a Shilling and a good Drink, and retir'd to my Quarters, where the civil Landlord gave me some Goose Pye, and some frigacied Rabbit.

In the Morning I survey'd the City, which I believe is the least in *England*, but surrounded by a very strong Wall. The Houses are very handsome, being fronted with smooth Stone, and the Streets very clean.

2. A colloquialism meaning that Moraley got drunk.
3. A draught of ale or some other alcohol.
4. An official who controlled the domestic affairs of the household.
5. A loaf of bread in the shape of a brick.

Leaving *Carlisle*, I directed my Course next towards *Corby Castle*, the Seat of a Gentleman nam'd *Howard*. In the Midway lies a Town belonging to the Earl of *Carlisle*, called *Torkat*, I lodg'd there all Night at an Ale-house, and had to Supper Goose Pye and hot Rice Milk. In the Morning, about Eleven or Twelve o'Clock, I discover'd *Corby Castle*, seated near the Banks of the River *Eden*. Adjoining to it are several Fields with many Relicks of Religious Worship, and in an Out Building an exceeding fine Chapel, the Altar adorn'd with several curious Ornaments.

I afterwards went into the Kitchen, where by the Fire-side, I saw all Sorts of the best Delicacies, such as Ducks, Geese, Pies, Puddings, Chickens, Jellies; in short, they put me in mind of the old *English* Hospitality. A young Lady, Daughter to Mr *Howard*, appear'd, and ask'd my Business; to which I answer'd, that being distress'd by Shipwreck, I was necessitated to ask Charity of well disposed Christians. She immediately went to her Father, who sent me Half a Crown.

But the Lady calling out for Mr *Ridley*, the Butler, to bring in more Wine, I took the Opportunity of changing my Name; and the Butler discharging his Duty, came back, and ask'd me my Name, which I said was *Ridley*. He hearing this, ask'd me of what Family I deriv'd my Pedigree; to which I reply'd, from *Willemoteswick*, and deduced my Descent from these Marriages spoken of before. I likewise told him, that being of the *Romish* Religion, my Parents discarded me, which oblig'd me to seek my Fortune. The Design taking, he gave me a Half Crown, and two Glasses of White Wine; so I left him to chew on the Cud, and departed.

The next Place I visited was *Warwick Hall*, the Seat of a Family so call'd; but the Gentleman being abroad, I was disappointed, and went towards *Haltwhistle*, and pass'd over *Coal Fell*, a dismal Place, where I met with no one Person to inform me how to proceed. This barren Place put me in mind of Mount *Atlas* and *Causacus*; for look which Way you will, you shall see nothing but Hill over Hill. After three Hours I discover'd *Haltwhistle*, and arrived at a little lone House near the Boundaries of the two Counties, where I was known, and treated with Goose Pye, and Wheaten Bannock[6] and Milk.

From thence I went to *Haltwhistle*, and quarter'd at *Barbara Bell's*, and the next Morning went to *Crow Hall*, formerly the Seat of the *Ridleys*, where I was known; from which I had a Sight of *Willemoteswick*

6. A type of bread.

Castle. I left *Crow Hall,* and pass'd over *Hayton Bridge,* and so towards *Hexham*; but about two Miles from it, I was belated, and lost in a Fell. It rain'd, and the Wind blew terribly hard. Here I thought my Condition was as bad as in *America*; but I soon discovered an old House, which I made up to, and desir'd Admittance. The People observing the Badness of my Attire did not readily comply with my Request; but a Man asking my Name, which having told him, he said he would admit me, because he had once a friend of that Name, whom I soon persuaded him was my Father's Brother. I had some Milk and Bread for Supper, but for a Bed I was obliged to lye with the Cows in the Byer[7] under the House, upon a little Straw, and with a shabby Coverlid.[8]

In the Morning he rous'd me up, and conducted me through a Wood, opposite to *Sandhoe,* to *Hexham,* where I left him, and enquir'd for Mr *John Ridley,* Brother to the Chief of that Family. He liv'd at *Battle Hill.* I knock'd at the Door, which his Wife open'd, and I ask'd, If her Husband was at home? Her Answer was, What Business have you with him! Tell him, Madam, said I, I am a Relation to him. You a Relation to him! said she, and so shut to the Door, and I was forced to trudge forward on my Journey.

From thence I pass'd over *Corbridge,* and baited at the *Golden Angel*; then went through *Ovingham,* then *Wylam,* and at length got to *Newburn,* where my Feet began to bleed: But remembering I had an old Friend, Mrs *Capstack,* I met with a handsome Reception; and so march'd towards home. I was ever looking for St *Nicolas* Church Steeple with the greatest Impatience, but did not discover till I came to the *Quarry House.* So passing by my Father's House, it being shut up, I went to Mr *Moraley's,* who lived then in the *Bigg-market,* where I met with a very kind Reception, and continued there three Weeks; after which I liv'd with my Mother till her Death, which happen'd about three Years and some Months after. Since that time I have experienc'd the greatest Misfortune, occasion'd by the Mistake of her Executors,[9] which is briefly as follows.

7. A "byre" is a cow-house or shed.

8. A covering of any kind.

9. The persons appointed by Moraley's mother to execute her will. The wills of Moraley's parents are reprinted in Appendix C.

POSTSCRIPT: THE AUTHOR'S CASE, RECOMMENDED TO THE GENTLEMEN OF THE LAW.

MY Mother had made a Will, and the Persons she appointed her Executors, seiz'd her Effects and Freehold, without an Administration granted them, and in conformity to her Will; of which they denied me a Copy, sold the Personal Effects, and refus'd to give me an Inventory of them. I endeavour'd to persuade them my Father's Will was never prov'd by her, and a Letter from *London* was produc'd to make my Assertion good, but all in vain. I was advis'd to have a Monition read at St *John's* Church, which was done, but the Executors never appear'd; tho' to prevent my Plea, which was *Bona Notabilia*, they procured Administration by unfair Practices, for which they charg'd me £4. An eminent Attorney procur'd a Copy of my Father's Will, and made it appear my Mother was only Tenant for Life, by the Custom of the City of *London*, tho' she mortgaged it for Fifty Pound, without my Knowledge.

If a Father is a Freeman of London, he cannot devise the Disposition of the Body of Infant, by the Statute of 12 Car. II &c. if he do, yet the Infant shall remain in the Custody of the Mayor and Aldermen; and this Custom, to have the Custody of the Orphans Person, of his Real and Personal Estate, extends to Lands out of London, SID.363. —And, *The Children of a Freeman may exhibit a Bill in the Lord Mayor's Court of Equity, having a Discovery of their Father's Estate, and for the Recovery of their Part, by the Custom of* London.[1]

I soon after seiz'd the Freehold; but the Executor procured a Warrant from a Justice of the Peace to shew cause why I shou'd not be imprison'd for dispossessing them; but I was released upon a Promise given, that I would not disturb them. I dispossessed them again; then Ejectments were served both against me and them, and the Executors told me, the Mortgagee was upon prosecuting them for not making Payment out of the personal Goods. Upon which I agreed to make a Sale of the House, purely to make them easy, by preventing a Law Suit.

But first we had a Meeting, in order to settle the Accounts of the Money arising from the Sale of Goods, when the Executors produced the Sum Total, which was Two Hundred and Six Pound; but afterwards they produced another of Seventy Three Pound short of the First; since which, I could never obtain either of the former Accounts. I was told, if I would release them, they would deliver me the remaining Effects, which I did, but have never received those Effects.

I was after this arrested for a small Debt, and in Custody of a Serjeant, but delivered by the Assistance of two Gentlemen, who paid the Charges. I afterwards convey'd the Freehold for One Hundred and Sixty Pound, which cost Five Hundred and Ten Pound, out of which I paid in my own Wrong Eighty-one Pound, and received only Seventy-nine Pound. At the Conveyance I demanded the Mortgage Deed and Security to be delivered up, but was refused, and threatened, by a Person present, if I did not immediately make a Conveyance, he would arrest me for the Debt I owed him. The Fear of a Prison, rather than any other Consideration, compelled me to the Sale.

Having paid all my Debts with the Money received, the Remainder was very inconsiderable; so that I am obliged at present to follow the meanest Imploy for a Subsistance, and shall endeavour to perswade the World to have a better Opinion of me than to think, that any Necessity shall compel me to act any otherwise than what is consistent with my Duty to God and my Neighbour; being sensible, whatever Hardships I

1. Appendix C explains the legal matters concerning Moraley's inheritance and reproduces the wills of his father and mother.

may lie under in this Life, tho' ever so afflicting, that they are infinitely preferrable to an Estate got by illegal Means; for tho' ill Persons may and do thrive for a While; yet a Time will come that will bring to light the hidden Things of Darkness,[2] when every one will be rewarded according to his Works.

I shall also endeavour, by my future Conduct, to make my Life easy under my unhappy Circumstance, by an entire Resignation to the Will of Providence, who has supported me thro' so many dangerous and tempestuous Seas of Adversity, and brought me safe to Land, where I continue, by the generous Assistance of the humane Inhabitants, a living Monument of God's Mercy.

FINIS.

2. 1 Corinthians 4:5–6: "Therefore judge nothing before the time, until the Lord come, who both will bring to light the hidden things of darkness, and will make manifest the counsels of the hearts: and then shall every man have praise of God. . . . Learn in us not to think of men above that which is written, that no one of you be puffed up for one against another."

EDITORS' AFTERWORD

William Moraley's narrative provides a remarkable perspective on life in America during the early decades of the eighteenth century. Moraley recounts both an adventure and a morality tale, even if the messages are somewhat ambiguous, even contradictory at points. He emphasizes that people usually bear responsibility for their own destinies, yet he also believes in the random, irrational influences of blind fate and the vicissitudes of fortune in human affairs. While admitting that he should have employed his talents to "improve 'em to a better Purpose" (4), he still perceives himself as the helpless, hapless "Tennis-ball of Fortune" (72).[1]

The tension between these perspectives gives rise to many of Moraley's incongruities and inconsistencies and reflects the important transition occurring between the seventeenth and eighteenth centuries in Britain and North America. Birth, rank, and the authority of superiors largely decide human destiny in a more "traditional" world in which chance, external

---

1. Numbers in parentheses refer to page numbers of Moraley's autobiography as reproduced in this volume.

circumstance, and divine providence play significant roles. In the second, more "modern" world of the emerging bourgeoisie, individuals, through their own intelligence, enterprise, and initiative, can take advantage of freedoms and opportunities to carve out careers and to control their own lives.

Moraley alternates between being the didactic moralist and the unapologetic rogue, like many heroes in contemporary fiction. He sometimes lacks the concern for prudent, restrained behavior associated with the middle class. Yet, compared to the cruelties and gratuitous violence presented in many rogue tales of the day, Moraley makes a very tame, respectable, even domesticated scoundrel. Moraley's charm is as evident as his blemishes in the memoir, and his portrayal of his own ambivalent character and attitudes makes his self-portrait all the more human.

Separating fact from fiction in Moraley's autobiography is particularly important since imaginary adventure tales were quite popular in England, and because Moraley obviously enjoyed spinning yarns. Indeed, like the genre of "beggar tales" that appeared in the nineteenth century, Moraley might have honed his stories by telling them aloud many times before committing them to paper.[2] He admits his pleasure in "wonderfully magnifying every Thing" (78) in describing the English king to Native Americans, and he certainly embellishes a few parts of his autobiography in a similar fashion. Moreover, while Moraley appears in records in England, only circumstantial evidence confirms his presence in New Jersey and Pennsylvania.[3]

How valid, then, is this account? The two stories Moraley inserts about Spaniards who convert to the Anglican faith are undoubtedly fanciful, although they may contain some basis in fact and may be related to his own life. One customer of Moraley's father around 1720 was a London merchant named William Morley, perhaps a relative. Morley had business

---

2. For a discussion of Daniel Defoe's influence on imaginary travel adventures, see Percy G. Adams, *Travelers and Travel Liars, 1669–1800* (Berkeley and Los Angeles: University of California Press, 1962), 105–17. See also R. W. Frantz, *The English Traveller and the Movement of Ideas, 1660–1732* (Lincoln: University of Nebraska Press, 1967); and Ann Fabian, *Beggars and Books* (Worcester, Mass.: American Antiquarian Society, 2000).

3. Moraley was far from unique in leaving no trace in the surviving sources. Many records do not exist for this early period, in part because the primitive conditions of New Jersey and Pennsylvania discouraged recordkeeping. For example, detailed censuses, registers of the arrivals of British migrants, city directories, and newspapers from New Jersey are not extant. Sharon V. Salinger found that 44 percent of male indentured servants in early Pennsylvania left no tracks in the records; *"To Serve Well and Faithfully": Labor and Indentured Servants in Pennsylvania, 1682–1800* (Cambridge: Cambridge University Press, 1987), 119.

accounts in the important Spanish towns of Cadiz, Seville, and Málaga; he also may have had kin in Spain, since he owed £200 to a cousin—who had the decidedly non-English name of Sancta Morley. Through this connection, William Moraley may have heard romantic tales of parental interference, intermarriage, and conversion, although similar tales were common at the time. The merchant Morley was also a director of the South Sea Company and undoubtedly encouraged Moraley's father to engage in disastrous speculations in that corporation's stock.[4] Even if the stories about Spain were fiction, Moraley's choice of Spanish themes may reflect significant events in his life.

A few of Moraley's others assertions are of doubtful veracity, especially his account of his trip to New York in the late summer of 1734. He claims to have enlisted in the British army there to escape his creditors while simultaneously serving as personal servant to a Spanish gentleman. However, he returns to New Jersey without being pursued for desertion from the army. This all seems quite unlikely and no other portion of Moraley's autobiography rings so false.

His memoir is otherwise subject to the same cautious reading that is required for all historical documents. Moraley commits errors in dating events (which are corrected in the footnotes) in part because he wrote a decade after the incidents he describes, in part because he sometimes wrote as events came to his mind, rather than recording his adventures in strict chronological order. Like many contemporaries in an age of faulty maps and nonexistent censuses, Moraley consistently overstates physical distance and population size. He is also often gullible by modern standards. His reports of freshwater sharks in the Delaware River, of the physiology of snakes and skunks, of the origin of fossil bones, and of the upper limits of the Delaware River are examples of local lore, rather than deliberate attempts to deceive.

Still, Moraley is most often a credible reporter. Various historical sources support his memoir on many crucial points. Ecclesiastical, guild, and public records in England confirm his birth, burial, apprenticeship, and indenture. Philadelphia newspapers verify the arrival and departure of

4. See "A Particular and Inventory of All and Singular the Lands, Tenements, and Hereditaments, Goods, Chattels, Debts, and Personal Estate Whatsoever, of William Morley, Esq." (London: Tonson, Lintot, and Taylor, 1721), 1, 2, 13, 14. This booklet was published as part of the bankruptcy proceedings and parliamentary investigation of the South Sea Company Directors that followed the bursting of the South Sea Bubble. The merchant had paid Moraley's father and another man £22.2.0 as part of the construction and furnishing of his new house in Charter-House Yard, London.

the ships that carried him to and from America, and an advertisement offers the sale of indentured servants by the owner of the vessel on which Moraley sailed (see Fig. 7). Moraley's depiction of scores of Mid-Atlantic inhabitants, both the relatively prominent and the lesser known, is likewise accurate. His account of the ghost in Isaac Pearson's home coincides with local Burlington court records, unpublished until the twentieth century. His anecdote about the witchcraft trial in Mount Holly agrees in most respects with Benjamin Franklin's description, although Moraley's report is more than a mere summary of Franklin's newspaper article. The wills left by Moraley's father and mother likewise support his own account of his financial and familial difficulties. In spite of the few instances of imaginative license, Moraley's own judgment of his work appears valid: "On the Whole, I have advanc'd nothing but what I know to be the Truth" (3).[5]

Moraley is more likely to omit significant events than he is to lie. This is especially true of the period between the remarriage of his mother on October 19, 1728 (three years after the death of his father), and his decision to sell himself into servitude a year later. Upon remarriage, Moraley's mother, like all married women, lost control of her property to her spouse—her new lord and master. Perhaps her husband refused to allow her to distribute what were now technically his assets to her son; maybe she herself tired of doling out money and used her new marriage as an excuse; possibly the newlyweds were simply absorbed in their own relationship. Whatever the family dynamics, Moraley was cast adrift, quickly became impoverished, and soon landed in Newcastle's Newgate Prison as

an insolvent debtor—an incident that he fails to mention in his autobiography.

Moraley's travails occurred during the national economic downturn of the 1720s, which hit Newcastle, already a depressed region with many unemployed people, especially hard. As poverty intensified, local judges condemned scores of residents who engaged in petty thefts of life's necessities (like a shirt or a piece of bread) to be whipped or to serve as bound

---

5. The advertisement offering indentured servants for sale is reproduced in Figure 15. The footnotes to Moraley's autobiography contain the citations for his indenture (chap. 1, n. 17); for the arrival and departure of the ships that carried Moraley to and from Philadelphia (chap. 3, n. 8 [see also Fig. 7] and chap. 10, n. 9, respectively); for Isaac Pearson (chap. 3, n. 11); for Sarah Pearson (chap. 5, n. 1); for residents of the Burlington area (chap. 5, nn. 3-7, chap. 7, nn. 22, 27; chap. 8, nn. 13, 14, 16); and for colonial officials (chap. 7, nn. 12, 16; chap. 8, n. 18). The legend about the ghost in Pearson's house is discussed in Appendix G; reports about the witchcraft "trial" are reprinted in Appendix H; and the wills of Moraley's father and mother are reproduced in Appendix C.

laborers in the "American plantations" for seven years. Responding to the national crisis, Parliament proclaimed a general amnesty for debtors, thereby freeing Moraley and sixty other Newcastle residents from prison and from the demands of their creditors at the end of May 1729.[6] The amnesty did not provide needed employment, however.

Ships routinely sailed the three-hundred-mile trip between Newcastle and London, and Moraley, perhaps legally forced to return to his place of nativity, apparently made the trip to London shortly after his prison release. London officials arrested him on June 23, leveling the charge of simple grand larceny for the theft of a "bushel and a half of Wheaten Flour." If the charge were true, Moraley must have been desperately hungry. Incarcerated until his case came to trial at the court of Old Bailey on July 9, Moraley won acquittal, "the Evidence against the Prisoner not being Sufficient."[7] Moraley also neglects to reveal this incident in his memoir. This encounter with the law may have put him in contact with the attorney who shortly afterward threatened a lawsuit against Moraley's mother for not providing him with more of his father's estate. Moraley does not say how he managed to survive for the next three months, but he was nearly starving by the time he signed his indenture and prepared to go overseas as a "voluntary Slave." His financial plight in the late 1720s was thus far more desperate than Moraley portrays in his autobiography.

Moraley Returns to Newcastle upon Tyne

In 1734, after five years in America, Moraley returned to Newcastle, a city of about eighteen thousand inhabitants (roughly three times larger than Philadelphia). The region remained in economic transition and crisis. As

6. Keith Bates notes the close trade relations between Newcastle and London and Moraley's imprisonment for debt in *The Clockmakers of Northumberland and Durham* (Rohbury, Morpeth, Northumberland: Pendulum Publications, 1980), 12, 241. The list of those freed from prison under the provisions of the Insolvent Debtors Act appears in *The London Gazette*, #6782, May 27–May 31, 1729. John J. McCusker and Russell R. Menard summarize the studies of English business cycles in *The Economy of British America, 1607–1789* (Chapel Hill: University of North Carolina Press, 1985), 62–64.

7. *Old Bailey Proceedings*, "William Morley," July 9, 1729, Image 0003, at www.oldbaileyonline.org, accessed December 1, 2004. The records indicate that Moraley (spelled in the proceedings as Morley) lived in St. Margaret's Parish, Westminster. On the docket that same day and tried immediately after Moraley was Robert Ibel, from the same parish, who was charged with having stolen twenty bushels of wheaten flour in February; Ibel also won acquittal. There may have been some connection between the two men.

coal mining, shipbuilding, and glassmaking gradually became more important in the area, the financial profits earned from these enterprises were distributed unequally among the inhabitants. A small group of aristocrats, businessmen, and professionals was consolidating both economic and political power in the city. Reflecting the intensification of poverty, Newcastle constructed three new almshouses during the second quarter of the eighteenth century.

In years of dearth, like both 1740 and 1750, widespread hunger inspired rebellions. When corn prices escalated and merchants refused to sell it at a cost affordable to middling and poorer folk in 1740, crowds of people plundered granaries, stopped a ship from carrying food out of the region, attacked the Guildhall and drove out the mayor and Council, and destroyed the Town Court and chambers. Soldiers from a nearby town eventually quelled the riot, and authorities arrested forty people, condemning many to transportation to the American colonies as servants for seven years. Troops remained in the city for at least two more years to maintain the peace. In 1745, because of public "outrages" supposedly committed by destitute people (and perhaps connected to Bonny Prince Charlie's effort to restore the Stuart monarchy), magistrates ordered constables to arrest all vagrants in Newcastle and punished them with whipping, jail terms, and forced return to their home parishes. Violence continued during the 1750s, and in 1761 soldiers fired into five thousand insurgents, killing eighteen of them.[8]

Moraley once again was caught up in economic forces largely beyond his control. To make matters worse, Moraley's mother, seemingly distrusting her son, specified in her 1740 will that the three executors of her estate should liquidate the assets, purchase an annuity, and dispense a monthly allowance to her son for the rest of his life. This arrangement, however, did not provide adequate funds for Moraley to become an independent master clockmaker, a property owner, or a freeman of the town with voting rights. Disappointed with this arrangement, Moraley railed in his memoir against the ostensible "mistakes" committed by the executors. He admits that he twice seized his mother's house against the orders of the court, but he neglects to mention that on July 15, 1741, he was indicted

    8. Sydney Middlebrook, *Newcastle Upon Tyne: Its Growth and Achievement* (Newcastle upon Tyne: S. R. Publishers, 1968), 115–16, 124–25; John Brand, *History and Antiquities of the Town and County of Newcastle on Tyne* (London: B. White & Son, 1789), 520–23; Joyce Ellis, "Urban Conflict and Popular Violence in the Guildhall Riots of 1740 in Newcastle upon Tyne," *International Review of Social History* 25, part 3 (1980): 332–49.

on a charge of assault against Timothy Forster, one of the executors of Moraley's mother's will. The target of Moraley's attack was hardly accidental; Moraley was expressing his frustration and anger at one of the men he blamed for his financial problems. The Quarter Sessions Court held Moraley's case over for four consecutive meetings, through July 1742, then dropped the charges, because Moraley agreed to the sale of the house, but, as he claims, never recovered the full value of his mother's estate.[9] It is probably around this time that Moraley suffered a nervous breakdown, something he joked about later in life.

Moraley wrote and published his memoir within this context. It helps explain his desperation to earn money, if only to stay out of jail by posting bond and settling with Forster. In addition, Moraley apparently wished to redeem his reputation by explaining his legal problems to his neighbors and by making a plea for sympathy from the court, to which he had also promised his "good behaviour." The narrative's postscript notes his intention to "endeavour to perswade the World to have a better Opinion of me" (106). Moraley also may have wanted to thank his supporters and creditors. John Sanderson, a master watchmaker, had posted half of the £20 bond, while Richard Adamson, an innkeeper in Newcastle, had guaranteed the other half. It is likely that Moraley worked as a journeyman in Sanderson's shop near St. Nicholas's church, and perhaps he rented a room in Adamson's inn.[10]

Moraley may also have written his memoir to chastise his enemies. His expression of gratitude in the memoir's preface to the "Worthy Gentlemen of *Newcastle*" (3) may be deeply ironic. On the one hand, he may sincerely have been acknowledging them "for the many Favours they have bestow'd on me" (3), including bailing him out of jail. On the other hand, he might have been sarcastically lambasting the executors who impeded his inheritance of his mother's property, since he had "no other Way to retaliate

9. Quarter Sessions Order Book, 1735–43, 134, Tyne and Wear Archives, Newcastle upon Tyne. It was probably around this time that Moraley suffered a severe mental depression or nervous breakdown, which he twice alludes to in his 1754 satire (see below) but does not mention in the *Infortunate*. As serious as his financial condition remained, he could at least laugh at himself by the 1750s.

10. Sanderson and Adamson are listed as "supporters" in Moraley's case in the Quarter Sessions Order Book, 1735–43, p. 134; Sanderson also is identified in Bates, *Clockmakers of Northumberland and Durham*, 15. On December 24, 1749, a William Sanderson married a Mary Moraley at St. Andrews Church in Newcastle. Mary may have been William's cousin, the daughter of the Mr. Moraley of the Bigg Market mentioned in the autobiography, or, if a soured marriage or a paternity suit was another reason for William Moraley's department from Newcastle in circa 1728, she could have been his daughter. This marriage indicates, like Hogarth's depictions of artisan success, the interconnectedness of family and business in the eighteenth century.

them" (3). At the time, "retaliate" meant to repay for *either* an injury or a kindness, and Moraley may have deliberately chosen the word to express its dual meaning.[11] Moraley returned to this theme in his closing pages, pointedly remarking (and perhaps criticizing Forster) that his own hardships were "infinitely preferrable to an Estate got by illegal Means" (107).

Moraley published two additional works after his return to Newcastle, an indication that he was not desperately poor since authors were customarily required to pay for the cost of publication. "The Orphan, or Revived Fugitive, Humbly dedicated to the Right Hon. The Lord Mayor of London" (1753) has, unfortunately, not been located. It is probably yet another attempt to argue for overturning the terms of his mother's will, since Moraley and his lawyer hoped to bring his case to the London equity courts presided over by the Lord Mayor. In 1754, Moraley published a twelve-page pamphlet, "The Proceedings and Humours of a Late Election in the City of Sandburg, with an Authentick List of the Illustrious Personages Who Honoured it with their Presence . . ."[12] Fewer than two thousand words, it is a satire of the parliamentary election of 1754. Writing under the pseudonym William Thompson, Moraley creates an imaginary political community in Newcastle where commoners are exalted and aristocrats belittled, where an expanded electorate actually decides elections, and where the interests of the community are promoted by political candidates. Moraley mocks social hierarchies and the connivance of the official church in maintaining inequalities. He protests the absence of political rights in Newcastle and the contempt of the wealthy. He does this in the name of a diverse group of poor and middling residents who want respect as well as a more representative government and religious liberty. It is far more radical than anything in his first publication, but Moraley's ideas reflect, at least in part, his experiences in New Jersey and Pennsylvania, where religious toleration and a weaker elite produced a more fluid social structure, at least for those who were not bound laborers.

Other aspects of the final years of Moraley's life remain obscure. Because his last name was common in the region, it is nearly impossible to tell if he ever married or had children. Conceivably, he may have been the "labourer" who lived in Ravensworth, four miles from Newcastle, and

---

11. *Oxford English Dictionary* (London: Oxford University Press, 1970).

12. "The Proceedings and Humours of a Late Election in the City of Sandburg, with an Authentick List of the Illustrious Personages Who Honoured it with their Presence, Published at the Request of several Persons of Distinction, by Wm. Thompson, Gent." (Newcastle, 1754). The pamphlet survives in an apparently unique copy in the University of Iowa Special Collections, University of Iowa.

in 1755 paid the small sum of six pence to apprentice his son as a ropem-
aker for seven years. Perhaps he wed Ann Friend in Ravensworth in 1749;
maybe he took vows with Elizabeth Robeson in nearby Whickham in
1755. The most intriguing possibility is that he married Hannah Forster
in neighboring Whalton in 1757. Could that have been the widow or
daughter of Timothy Forster, the executor of Moraley's mother's estate?
Did Moraley thereby finally obtain the inheritance that he had so long
sought? Alternatively, did he fail to gain sufficient financial independence
ever to take a wife? Whatever the answer, William Moraley, watchmaker,
died and was buried not in a pauper's grave but in Newcastle's St. Nicholas churchyard on January 19, 1762, at the age of sixty-two. He left an
important literary legacy that helps illuminate the early years of the
American colonial project and the Atlantic World to which he belonged.[13]

13. The marriage records are in the Tyne and Wear Archives, Newcastle upon Tyne. Moraley's death
is recorded in Richardson, *The Local Historian's Table Book,* 2:104.

APPENDIXES

APPENDIX A: THE BOOK AND ITS AUTHOR

John White first printed Moraley's autobiography, probably at the author's own expense, in 1743 at Newcastle-upon-Tyne, England. The William L. Clements Library at the University of Michigan currently holds a copy of that edition, a photocopy of which provided the basis for the version reproduced here. John Wilson, a friend of the Moraley family, first purchased the Clements Library copy of the *Infortunate*. Subsequently, he sold his copy to Thomas Bell, who wrote a brief history of the volume based on an interview with Wilson:

> The following exceedingly rare publication was printed in Newcastle, by White, in 1743. [I]t was purchased at the Sale of the Library of the late Mr. John Rawling Wilson, who esteemed it, a work of the greatest rarity, and one, on which he set an uncommon Value. [N]ot only on account of its scarcity, but from an Interest he had felt in the Narrative, when a Child; Moraley having been known to, and esteemed by his parents; and in a Conversation I had with Wilson respecting him & this Work, he (Wilson) told me that the Narrative was undoubtedly true; that Moraley was of a highly respectable Family, but a spend-thrift;—and who, on his settling in Newcastle, contrived to make a livelihood as a Watch-maker, tho' an easy,

and good natured fellow, whose wants were few, and cares, less.—He died in January 1762 and was buried in St Nicholas ChurchYard.[1]

Bell also recounted his understanding of Moraley's life for the Newcastle local antiquarian, M. A. Richardson:

> January 19. [1762]—Buried, "William Morley, Watchmaker," (*St. Nicholas' Register.*) This singular individual, whose real name was Moraley, was of good family and the heir to a considerable paternal estate,[2] which was spent in reckless extravagance and eventually he had to make a living as a watchmaker in Newcastle: —He published in 1743, an account of various transactions which had occurred to himself, previous to that year, under the title of "The Unfortunate: or, the Voyage and Adventures of William Moraley of Moraley in Northumberland, Gent." The late Mr. J. R. Wilson, had a copy of this extremely scarce tract, which at his sale, was purchased by Mr. Thomas Bell, land-surveyor, a work abounding in extraordinary and romantic incidents, but which is understood to have been a faithful record of the circumstances of his early life.[3]

Bell's heirs sold the book to the Clements Library in 1925.[4] In 1884 the *Delaware County Republican* (Chester, Pa.) published the *Infortunate* in an abridged and expurgated version. This was an exact copy of a contemporary reprinting of the autobiography in the *Newcastle (Weekly) Chronicle* (1764–1953), which had divided the volume into chapters and had added chapter summaries. Copies of this truncated version survive at the New York Public Library and at the Historical Society of Pennsylvania, Philadelphia.

1. Manuscript sheet tipped into the University of Michigan William L. Clements Library copy of Moraley's autobiography and attributed to Thomas Bell. A copy of the book in the Newcastle Central Library contains the same information written in a different hand at the front of the volume. Another manuscript note in the Newcastle Library copy identifies this as a second, expanded edition of Moraley's memoirs. If true, no trace of an earlier version can be found.

2. This is inaccurate, because Moraley's father left young William a bequest of only 20 shillings and some watchmaker's tools. Bell may have meant that Moraley was heir apparent to a considerable fortune—which, in fact, he never received.

3. M. A. Richardson, *The Local Historian's Table Book, of Remarkable Occurrences, Historical Facts, Traditions, Legendary and Descriptive Ballads, etc., etc., Connected with the Counties of Newcastle-upon-Tyne, Northumberland and Durham,* 8 vols. (Newcastle-upon-Tyne: Richardson, 1841), 2 (pt. 1): 104.

4. B. D. Maggs and E. U. Maggs, *Bibliotheca Americana et Philippina,* pt. 4, no. 465 (London, 1925), 193.

APPENDIX B: MORALEY GENEALOGY

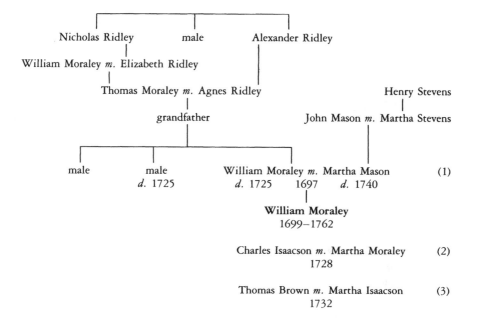

Note: All years have been converted to the new-style calendar, so William Moraley's birth, for example, is given here as 1699, although it was recorded as 1698. William Moraley was born February 25, 1699; baptized on March 1, 1699, at Christ Church, Greyfriars, Newgate; and buried on January 19, 1762, at St. Nicholas Church, Newcastle.

(1) William Moraley married Martha Mason on November 24, 1697, by virtue of a license from the Office of the Archbishop of Canterbury, London.

(2) Martha Moraley married Captain Charles Isaacson on October 19, 1728, at St. Andrew's, Newcastle.

(3) Martha Isaacson married Thomas Brown, armiger, on September 25, 1732, at South Shields, Durham.

APPENDIX C: THE WILLS OF
WILLIAM MORALEY'S PARENTS

Moraley's arguments in the Postscript (pp. 141–43) oversimplify the legal questions concerning the testamentary provision of his parents' wills. Contrary to his assertions, the wills of both of his parents were properly proven, in timely fashion, in the Consistory Court of the Archbishop of Durham, the appropriate jurisdiction for Newcastle. His mother's executors sold her effects, as mandated by her will, to purchase annuities for Moraley's support. The executors posted a £50 bond with the court to carry out the will of Martha Mason Moraley Isaacson Brown. The legal theory put forward by Moraley and his attorney was that his father's estate should have been probated in the Lord Mayor's Court in London because his father, as a member of the Clockmakers Company, was a freeman of London. This court was a court of equity, and it had the authority to overturn the specific provisions of the will and to order that one-third of the estate be provided for the support of the children of the descendant—that is, given to William Moraley. If his father's will were invalidated and the provisions of the intestate laws invoked, then his mother's will likewise would be nullified because she would have had no right to the entire property. Instead, she would have held the balance of the property as a tenant for life and consequently would have been barred from directing the disposal of her former husband's estate. In any event, the arguments became moot when Moraley forcibly seized the house, ejected the executors, and then agreed to the sale of the house to avoid both a lawsuit and imprisonment. His behavior at this juncture is puzzling, even irrational. Perhaps the pent-up frustration of forty-one years as a dependent—combined with the provisions of his mother's will, which would have kept him in dependency for the rest of his life—produced the events described in the final pages of his autobiography.[1]

Following are the wills of William Moraley's father and mother, currently located in the Archives of the Consistory Court of the Archbishop of Durham, Division of Archives and Special Collections, University Library, University of Durham, England. We have silently added punctuation. William Moraley did not leave a will at his own death in 1762.

Will of William Moraley's Father, Probated 1725

Know all men by these presents that I, William Moraley of the Towne of Newcastle upon Tyne in the County of Northumberland, Watch maker, in perfect health and Memory doth make my Last Will and Testament in Manner and forme following: that is to say when all my Debts and funerall charges is satisfied, which shall be with the Least Expence that can be—I give all my Estate both Reall and Personell unto My Dear and Beloved Wife Martha Moralay. Excepting my Working tools and twenty shilling in money which I give unto my Son William Moraley in order to gett his Living. [A]nd more over, by virtue of these presents, I doe Appoint my said Loving Martha Moraley My whole and sole Executrix of this my Last will and testament; as witness My hand and Seal the Eleventh day of November in the year of our Lord one thousand seven hundred and twenty five.

William Moraley

Signed Sealled & Published by Wm Morraley
as & for his last will & Testam[en]t in our presence
who in presence of the s[ai]d Wm Morraley
subscribed our names as wittnesses
        thereunto
                Ja[mes] Bell
                Tho[ma]s Armstrong
                Char[les] Smithson
                15. Martii 1725/6

1. We are indebted to Dr. J. M. Fewster, Senior Assistant Keeper, and Mrs. J. L. Drury, Assistant Keeper, of the Division of Archives and Special Collections of the University of Durham Library for their generous assistance in tracing and explaining the wills and court procedures.

Jurat fuer[un]t supranol[m]i[n]ata
Martha Moraley Vidua et Executrix
   ac Jacobus Bell Testis
         coram me
            Ed: Bell Sur[rogate]:

Will of William Moraley's Mother, Probated 1740

In the Name of God, Amen. I, Martha Brown of the Town and County of
Newcastle upon Tyne, Widdow, being infirm in Body but of Sound Per-
fect and disposeing Mind and Memory, Do think fit to make this my last
Will and Testament in manner and form following. First, I Comitt my
Soul to God who gave it, hopeing for the Pardon of all my Sins through
the Meritts and Satisfaction of my Blessed Saviour, and my body to the
Earth to be decently buryed according to the discretion of my Executors
hereafter Named. Next, I order and Appoint all my Just Debts and funerall
Expences to be fully satisfyed and paid. Item, I Do hereby Give, Devise
and bequeath unto James Bell of the Town and County of Newcastle upon
Tyne, Gentleman, Timothy Forster of Newcastle aforesaid, Surgeon, and
Thomas Watson of Newcastle aforesaid, Gentleman, And to their Heirs,
Executors, Administrators and assigns All my Messuage, Tenement or
dwelling house Wherein I now live and Garden thereunto adjoyning, together with All and Singular the rights, Members and Appurtenances
thereunto belonging; scituate, Standing, lying, and being, at or Near a
certaine place called the Firth, and also all my household Goods and Furniture, Plate, Rings, Watches and Personall Estate of what nature or kind
soever, which I shall be possessed of at the time of my Death upon Special
Trust and Confidence and to and for the Uses, Intents and purposes hereafter Mentioned: (that is to say) Upon Trust that they, the said James Bell,
Timothy Forster and Thomas Watson, their Heirs, Executors, Administrators and Assigns, Shall and do, so soon as Conveniently may be after my
decease, Sell, Convey and Dispose of all my said Messuage, Tenement or
Dwelling house, Garden and personall Estate for the best price that cann be
gotten for the Same; and after the said premises shall be so Sold shall and
do so soon as they conveniently can, lay out and Expend all such Sume and
Sumes of Money that shall arise by such sale after payment of my Debts
and funerall Expences in the purchaseing one or more Annuity or Annuities
in Money to be secured and made payable out of Lands, or by other good
Security, to the said James Bell, Timothy Forster and Thomas Watson,
their Heirs, Executors, Administrators and Assigns, as they the said James
Bell, Timothy Forster and Thomas Watson, their Heirs, Executors, Ad-

ministrators and Assigns shall approve of, for and dureing and unto the full end and Term of the Naturall Life of my beloved Son William Morley. And after the receiveing such Annuity or Annuities shall and do Devide and pay the same in eaqual Monthly Shares and Proportions, Yearly and ever Year, to my said Son, William Morley, for and dureing his Naturall Life; first deducting all such Charges and Expences As they the said James Bell, Timothy Forster and Thomas Watson, their Executors, Administrators, Heirs and Assigns shall Expend or be put to in the Execution and performance of the aforesaid Trust or any way relateing thereunto. Nevertheless, it is my Mind and Will and I Do order and Appoint that it shall and may be lawfull to and for the said James Bell, Timothy Forster and Thomas Watson, their Heirs, Executors, Administrators and Assigns untill such Annuity or Annuities shall be purchased as aforesaid to pay to my said Son out of the Sume or Sumes of Money ariseing by sale of my said reall or personall Estates or the Rents and profits such Weakly allowance or Maintenance as they shall think Necessary and Convenient.

Item, I give and bequeath unto my Sister Elizabeth Owton My best blew Silk damask Suit, My Green Tabby Suit of Cloths, and my White Night Gown together with the one halfe of my Body or wearing Linnen.

Item, I give and bequeath to my Servant Ann Kirkhouse All my other wearing Apparell, Cloths and Body or wearing Linnen. Item, I do hereby Name, Constitute and Appoint the said James Bell, Timothy Forster and Thomas Watson, Joynt Executors of this My Last Will and Testament, Revokeing and makeing Void All former and other Wills whatsoever by me at any time heretofore made. In Witness whereof I have hereunto sett my Hand and Seal this Twelvth day of November in the Twelvth Year of the Reign of our Soveraign Lord King George the second over Great Brittaine, France and Ireland and so forth, And in the Year of our Lord One thousand seven hundred thirty and Eight.

                                                         Martha Brown

Signed Sealed Published and Declared by the above Martha Brown for and as her last Will and Testament in the presence of us who in the presence and at the request of the above named Testatrix have hereunto suscribed our Names as Witnesses to the Executeing thereof

                                                         Henry Isaacson
                                                         John Airey
                                                         Mark Ogle

December the 17th 1740. Henry Isaacson a Subscribing Witness—was sworn to the due Execution hereof and Timothy Forster—One of the Ex-

ecutors herein nam'd was also Sworn well & truly—to Execute & perform
&c

>   before me
>   Tho[mas] Maddison
>   Surrogate

APPENDIX D: MORALEY AS A LITERARY ARTISAN

William Moraley's autobiography is suggestive about the reading habits of the English "middling sort" during the early eighteenth century. In it, Moraley alludes to a number of books, including Aesop's fables, the Bible, Dr. John Tillotson's "Rule of Faith," and the *Epistles* of Horace, which many adolescents first read in school. Moraley's familiarity with the Bible is apparent in his quotations from and references to the psalms and the New Testament. In addition to these books, Moraley read plays, novels, and poetry. Several public libraries provided Londoners with relatively easy access to books. And in the used-book market in Moorfields, "saunt'ring 'prentices" gathered at the stalls to read Restoration dramatists (Thomas Otway and William Congreve were favorites), while "Pleased semp-stresses" became engrossed in Alexander Pope's "Rape of the Lock."[1] Moraley twice included in his memoirs his own attempts at poetry, although both pieces built on the work of others. His prose is at times self-consciously poetic, as in "Then the green Fields and verdant Meadows display their several Beauties, advantageous to the joyful Shepherd" (107), although his writing generally resembles the more

---

1. John Gay, "Trivia; or, The Art of Walking the Streets of London" (1716), in *Poems of John Gay*, ed. John Underhill, 2 vols. (London: Routledge, 1893), 1:147–48.

straightforward style of Daniel Defoe. The title of Moraley's memoirs makes obvious reference to the literature of "unfortunates." These popular novels and autobiographies—*The Unfortunate General* (1713), *Unfortunate Heiress* (1726), *Unfortunate Dutchess* (1739), *Unfortunate Englishman* (1742), *Unfortunate Concubines* (1748), *Unfortunate Mother* (1761), and even another voyager to New Jersey and Pennsylvania, *The Unfortunate Husbandman* (1784)—focused on the lives and opinions of common men and women and reflected the new and expanding eighteenth-century reading public.

While in the colonies Moraley also read almanacs. George Webb's poem about Philadelphia, which appeared in Titan Leeds's *Almanac* for 1730, is reproduced below as an example of the type of poetry Moraley thought he could improve.[2] Moraley shortened, rearranged, and added a few lines to the original.

> Goddess of Numbers, who art wont to rove
> O'er the gay Landskip, or the smiling Grove;
> Who taught me first to sing in humble Strains,
> Of murm'ring Fountains, and of flowery Plains,
> Assist me now; while I in Verse repeat
> The heavenly Beauties of thy Fav'rite Seat.
>
> Teach me, O Goddess, in harmonious Lays,
> To sing thy much-lov'd *Pennsylvania's* Praise;
> Thy *Philadelphia's* Beauties to indite,
> In Verse as tuneful as her Sons can write:
> Such as from B———l's Pen are wont to flow,
> Or more judicious T———r's us'd to show.
>
> Stretch'd on the Bank of *Delaware's* rapid Stream
> Stands *Philadelphia*, not unkown to Fame:
> Here the tall Vessels safe at Anchor ride,
> And *Europe's* Wealth flows in with every Tide:
> Thro' each wide Ope the distant Prospect's clear;
> The well-built Streets are regularly fair:
>
> The Plan by thee contriv'd, O *Penn*, the Scheme,
> A Work immortal as the Founder's Name.
> 'Tis here *Apollo* does erect his Throne,
> This his *Parnassus*, this his *Helicon*:
> Here solid Sense does every Bosom warm,
> Here Noise and Nonsense have forgot to charm.

2. George Webb, in Titan Leeds, *The Genuine Leeds Almanac for . . . 1730* (Philadelphia: Leeds, 1730).

Thy Seers how cautious! and how gravely wise!
Thy hopeful Youth in Emulation rise:
Who (if the wishing Muse inspir'd does sing)
Shall Liberal Arts to such Perfection bring,
Europe shall mourn her ancient Fame declin'd,
And *Philadelphia* be the *Athens* of Mankind.

Thy lovely Daughters unaffected shine,
In each Perfection, every Grace divine:
Beauty triumphant sits in every Eye,
And Wit shines forth, but check'd with Modesty;
Decently Grave, which shows a sober Sense,
And Chearful too, a Sign of Innocence.

But what. O *Pennsylvania* does declare
Thy Bliss, speaks thee profusely happy: here
Sweet *Liberty* her gentle Influence sheds,
And *Peace* her downy Wings about us spreads:
While War and Desolation widely reigns,
And Captive Nations groan beneath their Chains.

While half the World implicitly obey,
Some lawless Tyrant's most imperious Sway
No threatning Trumpet warns us from afar
Of hastning Miseries or approaching War;
Fearless the Hind pursues his wonted Toil,
And eats the Product of his grateful Soil.

No unjust Sentence we have Cause to fear
No arbitrary Monarch rules us here.
Our Lives, our Properties, and all that's ours,
Our happy Constitution here secures.
What Praise and Thanks, O *Penn*! are due to thee!
For this first perfect Scheme of Liberty!

How shall the Muse thy just Applauses sing?
Or in what Strains due Acclamations bring?
Who can thy Charter read, but with Surprize
Must strait proclaim thee Generous, Just and Wise?
Thro' every Page, thro' every careful Line,
Now does the Friend, the Nursing Father shine!

What Toils, what Perils didst thou under go,
Thro' scorching Heats, thro' endless Tracts of Snow?
How scorning Ease didst tempt the raging Floods?

How hew thy Passage thro' untrodden Woods?
Thine was the Danger, Thine was all the Toil;
While We, ungrateful We, divide the Spoil.

O cou'd my Verse a Monument but raise,
Some Part, some little Sketch of thy due Praise,
When Time, the Tomb, or Statue shall destroy,
Or *Philadelphia's* Self in Dust shall lye,
Ages to come should read thy Favourite Name,
Fresh and immortal in the Book of Fame.

APPENDIX E: NEWCASTLE, ENGLAND

In 1723 the Moraley family moved from London, a metropolis of perhaps 750,000 people, to northeastern England's Newcastle-upon-Tyne, a substantially smaller town that contained approximately 18,000 inhabitants and was the ancestral home of the Moraleys.[1] Despite its smaller size, Newcastle, according to one visitor, "most resembles London of any place in England," in part because the "shops are good and of Distinct trades, not selling many things in one shop as is ye Custom in most Country towns and Cittys."[2] Family connections, a specialized retail economy, and a busy port made Newcastle a likely place to recoup the family's fortunes. Daniel Defoe vividly describes the town during the 1720s:

> From [Durham] the road to Newcastle gives a view of the inexhausted store of coals and coal pits, from whence not London only, but all the south part of England is continually supplied. . . . Newcastle is a spacious, extended, infinitely populous place; 'tis seated upon the River Tyne, which is here a noble, large and deep river, and ships of any reasonable burthen may come

---

1. P. M. Horsley, *Eighteenth-Century Newcastle* (Newcastle: Oriel, 1971), 220.
2. Celia Fiennes, *Through England on a Side Saddle* (London: Field & Tuer, 1888), 176–77.

safely up to the very town. . . . The situation of the town to the landward is exceeding unpleasant, and the buildings very close and old, standing on the declivity of two exceeding high hills, which, together with the smoke of the coals, makes it not the pleasantest place in the world to live in; but it is made amends abundantly by the goodness of the river, which runs between the two hills, and which, as I said, bringing ships up to the very quays, and fetching the coals down from the country, makes it a place of very great business. . . . They build ships here to perfection, I mean as to strength, and firmness, and to bear the sea; and as the coal trade occasions a demand for such strong ships, a great many are built here. This gives an addition to the merchants' business, in requiring a supply of all sorts of naval stores to fit out those ships. Here is also a considerable manufacture of hard ware, or wrought iron, lately erected after the manner of Sheffield, which is very helpful for employing the poor, of which this town has always a prodigious number.[3]

3. Daniel Defoe, *A Tour Through the Whole Island of Great Britain*, ed. Pat Rogers (Aylesbury, Eng.: Penguin, 1971), 535–37.

APPENDIX F: ISAAC PEARSON'S SERVANTS

Isaac Pearson, Moraley's master, advertised for three runaway servants in the newspapers between 1727 and 1737. The advertisement for the first escapee appeared in the March 30—April 6, 1727, edition of the *American Weekly Mercury*:

> Run away on the 3rd of this Instant April, from Isaac Pearson of Burlington, a Servant Man, he is a short well set Fellow, and Purblind, named ——— ——— about 30 Years of Age, round Visage, his Hair cut off; he has on an old Hat, a redish strip'd Cap, a dark Drugget Pea Jacket, and a striped Flannel Jacket with blue stripes under the same, a pair of Ozenbrig Drawers, and round Toed Shoes. Whoever secures the said Servant so that his Master may have him again, shall have 40 Shillings Reward and reasonable Charges.

Figure 17 reproduces the notice for Aaron Middleton, and Pearson advertised for a third servant in the August 25—September 1, 1737, issue of the *Pennsylvania Gazette*:

> Run away from Isaac Pearson, of Burlington, in West-New-Jersey, a Servant Man named John Williams, aged about 37 Years, a West-Country

Man, speaks by Clusters, hard to understand, very short, square set, by Trade a Clockmaker: He had on a full-trimm'd brown colour'd cloth Coat, with flat Pearl Buttons set in Brass, a flannel strip'd Jacket with blue Flaps, a fine Shirt, and an Ozenbrigs one, ozenbrigs Trousers, blue worsted Stockings, peaked toe'd Shoes, with Hobnails drove in the Heels, a narrow brim'd castor Hat.

Whoever secures the said Servant so that he may be had again, shall have Thirty Shillings Reward, paid by Isaac Pearson.

APPENDIX G: THE GHOST IN
ISAAC PEARSON'S HOME

In 1686 a notorious case had occurred in what would be Moraley's residence in Burlington. James Wills was indicted for murdering his African bondswoman. One witness at the trial heard noises "and supposed it to be James Wills beating his Negro woman, and heard many Lashes more and Crying out, untill hee was greevd and went into his owne house and shut the dore, and said to his wife oh! yond cruell man, and sayth hee beleeves hee heard full a hundred stripes or lashes." Despite similar testimony from other witnesses, Wills was acquitted on the grounds that the unnamed woman died from long-standing health problems rather than from the beating.[1] Isaac Pearson purchased the Wills estate on the west side of High Street in 1715.[2]

Many if not most seventeenth- and eighteenth-century Europeans and Americans believed in ghosts. One element of most ghost stories was that the apparition

1. H. Clay Reed and George J. Miller, *The Burlington Court Book: A Record of Quaker Jurisprudence in West New Jersey, 1680–1709* (Washington, D.C.: American Historical Association, 1944), 56–57. For a further discussion of this case, see Ernest Lyght, *Path of Freedom: The Black Presence in New Jersey's Burlington County, 1659–1900* (Cherry Hill, N.J.: E & E Publishing, 1978).

2. Robert Thompson, City of Burlington Historic Commission (Typed memo, March 4, 1986, in "Pearson-How House File," Burlington County Historical Society).

always had a specific reason for appearing. A popular superstition in and around Newcastle, England, held that "though justice should fail in detecting the murderer, yet went he not without punishment even on earth, for not unfrequently did the spirit of his victim appear to him in the darkness and solitude of night, filling his mind with terror, to which death would have been to him a relief, had he not dreaded the greater torments which awaited him hereafter."[3]

3. On the belief in ghosts in early modern England and America, see Keith Thomas, *Religion and the Decline of Magic* (New York: Charles Scribner's Sons, 1971), 587–99. Quotation from Richardson, *The Local Historian's Table Book*, 1 (pt. 2): 34.

APPENDIX H: THE WITCHCRAFT TRIAL
AT MOUNT HOLLY

Only two accounts of the witchcraft "trial" at Mount Holly, New Jersey, survive. The article published in the *Pennsylvania Gazette* by Benjamin Franklin, which he may or may not have authored, is considered a "hoax" by the editors of Franklin's papers.[1] But Moraley offers a second report, which seemingly confirms many of its details. The stories share a number of similarities: two people were accused; the tests consisted of both weighing the suspects against the Bible and floating them on water; and the two ordeals failed to prove demonic possession. At one point the language of the two versions is virtually identical. Moraley observed that "to the Surprise of the Beholders, [the suspects] weighed down both Prophets and Apostles" (124), while Franklin's article stated that "to the great Surprize of the Spectators, . . . [the accused] were too heavy for *Moses* and all the Prophets and Apostles." Moreover, both reporters were extremely skeptical of the proceedings.

Yet the two accounts contain several discrepancies. Moraley dated the trial as taking place in September 1734, four years after the newspaper story. He simply may have forgotten to describe the episode in the proper sequence while writing

1. Leonard W. Labaree and Whitfield J. Bell Jr., eds., *The Papers of Benjamin Franklin* (New Haven: Yale University Press, 1959–), 1:182.

his memoirs and, rather than rewrite the draft, decided to sidetrack himself in his narrative in order to recount the event. Moraley identified the suspects as two elderly women whose facial features had made them suspicious, while the *Gazette* specified that the accused were a man and a woman who had enchanted local barnyard animals.

It is doubtful that Moraley merely retold the story based on his hazy recollection of Franklin's newspaper article, because Moraley, unlike the newspaper, identified Jonathan Wright as the local justice who presided over the trial. And Wright, an influential and wealthy Quaker, was a good candidate for the role. In 1713 he moved from Chesterfield to Burlington, where he resided until his death in 1742, at which time he owned 1,600 acres of land, several improved lots, and a tanyard. Wright served repeatedly as the local representative to the quarterly meeting of the Quakers and participated actively in town politics and in judicial affairs on the county level. Moreover, Wright did fit the description in the newspaper article. He had a wife, Elizabeth Fretwell, in 1730; he was a county constable beginning in 1719; and he was commissioned Justice of the Peace in 1732 and may well have served in that capacity previously. According to his will, Wright also owned "a large quarto Bible,"[2] perhaps not unlike the one used in the trial. Whether Wright was also a "grave tall Man," as Franklin's story specified, is unknown.

Wright may have been induced to stage this mock trial, not to prosecute witches but to acquit the innocent victims of popular prejudice in response to the following petition, which was in circulation among Burlington Quakers prior to 1730:

> Please your Worships, gentlemen. Pray doe have some Charety for me, a
> poor Distrest man that is become old and scars able to Mentain my Famely
> at the best, and now sum Peopel has raised a Reporte that my Wife is a
> Witch, by which I and my famely must sartinly suffer if she cant be clear'd
> of the thing and a Stop Poot to the Reporte for Peopel will not have no
> Delings with me on the acount[.] Pray Gentlemen I beg the favor of you
> that one or more of you would free her for she is Desirous that she may be
> tried by all Maner of Ways that ever a Woman was tried so that she can get

2. William Wade Hinshaw, *Encyclopedia of American Quaker Genealogy*, 9 vols. (Richmond, Ind.: Edwards, 1938), 2:249; Henry H. Bisbee and Rebecca Bisbee Colesar, eds., *The Burlington Town Book, 1694–1785* (Burlington, N.J.: Bisbee, 1975); Wills, 2:550; Larry C. Wright, *Wright's 400 Years-Plus: Thirteen Generation Family* (Amarillo, Tex.: Wright, 1984), 12–18; George Gates Radden Jr., comp., "The Wrights of West New Jersey," 3 vols. (Manuscript in the James Duncan Philips Library of the Essex Institute Library, Salem, Mass., 1953–63), 1:19; Minutes of the Burlington Monthly Meeting, Burlington County Historical Society.

Wright fell from grace in 1739 when he was disowned by the meeting for reasons that had nothing to do with witchcraft, and his attempts to gain reinstatement failed.

Cleare of the Report[.] from your poor and Humble Servant, Jeames Moore.[3]

This petition supports the newspaper's contention that the accused voluntarily appeared and were desirous of a trial, as well as Moraley's claim that it was the facial features of old women that brought them the reputation of witchery.

Indeed, it is possible that Moraley, who was living in Mount Holly in 1730, acted as the source for the newspaper article. This could account for the article's two London references: "after the Manner of *Moorfields*" and "as solemnly as the Sword-bearer of *London* before the Lord Mayor."[4] Another explanation is that the newspaper account helped shape contemporary gossip about the event. The newspaper piece from the October 15–22, 1730, issue of the *Pennsylvania Gazette* follows.

BURLINGTON, Oct. 12. Saturday last at *Mount-Holly*, about 8 Miles from this Place, near 300 People were gathered together to see an Experiment or two tried on some Persons accused of Witchcraft. It seems the Accused had been charged with making their Neighbours Sheep dance in an uncommon Manner, and with causing Hogs to speak, and sing Psalms, &c. to the great Terror and Amazement of the King's good and peaceable Subjects in this Province; and the Accusers being very positive that if the Accused were weighed in Scales against a Bible, the Bible would prove too heavy for them;[5] or that, if they were bound and put into the River, they would swim;[6] the said Accused desirous to make their Innocence appear, voluntarily offered to undergo the said Trials, if 2 of the most violent of their Accusers would be tried with them. Accordingly the Time and Place was agreed on, and advertised about the Country; The Accusers were 1

3. Quoted in Amelia Mott Gummere, *Witchcraft and Quakerism: A Study in Social History* (Philadelphia: Biddle, 1908), 56.

4. A popular gathering place, "Moorfields" was an area near the outskirts of London just north of the guild hall, royal exchange, and other locales associated with Moraley and his family. The solemnity of the "Sword-bearer of *London* before the Lord Mayor" refers to the manner in which he proceeded, described as follows: "When the Mayor goes out of the precincts of the City a sceptre, a sword, and a cap are borne before him, and he is followed by the principal Aldermen in scarlet gowns with gold chains, himself and they on horseback" (Walter Besant, *London in the Time of the Stuarts* [London: Black, 1903], 334).

5. Because witches assumed spectral shapes, the Bible, as a literally and figuratively substantial book of God, would outweigh insubstantial witches. See Marion L. Starkey, *The Devil in Massachusetts* (New York: Time Inc., 1949), 37ff.

6. The following observation about witches by James I was a popular belief: "God hath appoynted (for a super-naturell signe of the monstrous impietie of Witches) that the water shall refuse to receive them in her bosom, that have shaken off them the sacred water of Baptisme" (as quoted in R. Trevor Davies, *Four Centuries of Witch Beliefs* [London: Methuen, 1947], 47).

Man and 1 Woman; and the Accused the same. The Parties being met, and the People got together, a grand Consultation was held, before they proceeded to Trial; in which it was agreed to use the Scales first; and a Committee of Men were appointed to search the Men, and a Committee of Women to search the Women, to see if they had any Thing of Weight about them, particularly Pins.[7] After the Scrutiny was over, a huge great Bible belonging to the Justice of the Place was provided, and a Lane through the Populace was made from the Justices House to the Scales, which were fixed on a Gallows erected for that Purpose opposite to the House, that the Justice's Wife and the rest of the Ladies might see the Trial, without coming amongst the Mob; and after the Manner of *Moorfields*, a large Ring was also made. Then came out of the House a grave tall Man carrying the Holy Writ before the supposed Wizard, &c. (as solemnly as the Sword-bearer of *London* before the Lord Mayor) the Wizard was first put in the Scale, and over him was read a Chapter out of the Books of *Moses*,[8] and then the Bible was put in the other Scale, (which being kept down before) was immediately let go; but to the great Surprize of the Spectators, Flesh and Bones came down plump, and outweighed that great good Book by abundance. After the same Manner, the others were served, and their Lumps of Mortality severally were too heavy for *Moses* and all the Prophets and Apostles. This being over, the Accusers and the rest of the Mob, not satisfied with this Experiment, would have the Trial by Water; accordingly a most solemn Procession was made to the Mill-pond; where both Accused and Accusers being stripp'd (saving only to the Women their Shifts) were bound Hand and Foot, and severally placed in the Water, lengthways, from the Side of a Barge or Flat, having for Security only a Rope about the Middle of each, which was held by some in the Flat. The Accuser Man being thin and spare, with some Difficulty began to sink at last; but the rest every one of them swam very light upon the Water. A Sailor in the Flat jump'd out upon the Back of the Man accused, thinking to drive him down to the Bottom; but the Person bound, without any Help, came up some time before the other. The Woman Accuser, being told that she did not sink, would be duck'd a second Time; when she swam again as light as before. Upon which she declared, That she believed the

---

7. Witches commonly used domestic items like pins as weapons; see Carol F. Karlsen, *The Devil in the Shape of a Woman: Witchcraft in Colonial New England* (New York: Vintage, 1987), 6–14.

8. See the Fifth Book of Moses, Deuteronomy 18:10–12: "There shall not be found among you *any one* that maketh his son or his daughter to pass through the fire, or that useth divination, or an observer of times, or an enchanter, or a witch, or a charmer, or a consulter with familiar spirits, or a wizard, or a necromancer. For all that do these things are an abomination unto the Lord: and because of these abominations the Lord thy God doth drive them out from before thee."

Accused had bewitched her to make her so light, and that she would be duck'd again a Hundred Times, but she would duck the Devil out of her. The accused Man, being surpriz'd at his own Swimming, was not so confident of his Innocence as before, but said, *If I am a Witch, it is more than I know.* The more thinking Part of the Spectators were of Opinion, that any Person so bound and plac'd in the Water (unless they were mere Skin and Bones) would swim till their Breath was gone, and their lungs fill'd with Water. But it being the general Belief of the populace, that the Womens Shifts, and the Garters with which they were bound help'd to support them; it is said they are to be tried again the next warm Weather, naked.

INDEX

Adamson, Richard, 115
Africa, xxi, xxxvii, 37–40, 52
African Americans, xx, xxii, xxxvii, xxxiv, 78. *See also* slaves and slavery
agriculture. *See* farms and farmers
alcoholic beverages. *See* Moraley, William, *under* condition, drink; Pennsylvania, *under* customs, drink
Allentown, N.J., 76
Almeria, Don Roderigo de, 79–87
Alsop, George (1636?–1673?), xl
America (North), xii, xxiii, xxv, xvii–xxi, xxx, xxxvi, xxxvii, xli, 109
American dream. *See* class; mobility, social
Anglicans. *See* Church of England
animals. *See* birds; fish; insects; wildlife; *names of specific animals*
Anne, Queen (r. 1702–14), 33, 79
Apess, William (1798–1839), xxxix, xl
apprenticeship. *See* artisans
aristocracy, xxii, 51, 114, 116
army and militias, British, 32, 35, 78–79
army, French, 18–19
artisans. xviii, xx, xxiii, xxvii, xxix–xxxii, 115. *See*

also clockmakers and watchmakers; Moraley, William, work
apprentices, xviii, xxiv, xxv
demand for in colonies, 16, 53
wages, 53
Ashbridge, Elizabeth Sampson (1713–1755), xxxix–xl
Atlantic World, xxi–xxii, xxxv, xxxvii, 117

Bailis. *See* Baylis, Robert
Banish'd Duke, The (1690), 2
battles. *See* warfare
Baylis, Robert (fl. 1729), 16, 16 n. 21
bees, honey, 56–57
Behn, Alphra, xxxix
Bell, James (fl. 1740), 127–28
Bell, Thomas, 121–22
Bennet, Richard (1666–1749), 91, 91 n. 5
Biddle, Charles (1745–1821), xl
birds, 26, 53, 56
eagles, bald, 49, 56–57, 93
gannets, 95
geese, 48, 93–94
hummingbird, 55